Gregory W. Yasinitsky

Improvisation 101: Major, Minor and Blues

advance music | improvisation

Gregory W. Yasinitsky

Improvisation 101: Major, Minor and Blues

A Step-by-Step Approach to Improvisation in Jazz, Rock and Pop Music
Der Weg zum freien Spiel in Jazz, Rock und Pop

for B♭ instruments
für Instrumente in B♭

www.advancemusic.com | © 2016 advance music GmbH, Mainz | Printed in Germany

Deutsche Übersetzung: Heike Brühl
Covergestaltung: Schultz & Schultz Mediengestaltung, Wien
© 2016 advance music GmbH, Mainz
Printed in Germany

ADV 14411
ISMN 979-0-2063-1017-1
ISBN 978-3-95481-039-0

Table of Contents

Improvising in Key Centers 7
    Four Tips for New Improvisers 7

About the Recordings 8
    The Musicians 8
    Play-Along Recordings 9
    Rhythm Section 9
    Improvised Solos 9

1 **"Getting Started"** 10
    What to Play | Why This Works |
    About the Harmony | In Major Keys 10
    Lead Sheet | Improvised Solos 12

2 **"A Minor Change"** 15
    What to Play | Why This Works |
    Another Option | About the Harmony |
    In Minor Keys 15
    Lead Sheet | Improvised Solos 17

3 **"The Key"** 20
    What to Play | Why This Works |
    About the Harmony | In Major Keys 20
    Lead Sheet | Improvised Solos 22

4 **"It's All Relative"** 25
    What to Play | Why This Works |
    Another Option | About the Harmony 25
    Lead Sheet | Improvised Solos 27

5 **"C Note"** 30
    What to Play | Why This Works |
    Another Option | About the Harmony |
    In Minor Keys 30
    Lead Sheet | Improvised Solos 32

6 **"Blue Riff"** 35
    What to Play | Why This Works |
    About the Harmony 35
    Lead Sheet | Improvised Solos 38

7 **"Blue Funk"** 41
    What to Play | Why This Works |
    About the Harmony 41
    Lead Sheet | Improvised Solos 43

8 **"Feelin' Blue"** 46
    What to Play | Why This Works |
    About the Harmony 46
    Lead Sheet | Improvised Solos 48

Inhalt

Improvisieren in tonalen Zentren 7
    Vier Tipps für Improvisationsneulinge 7

Die Aufnahmen 8
    Die Musiker 8
    Playalong-Aufnahmen 9
    Rhythmusgruppe 9
    Improvisierte Solos 9

1 **„Getting Started"** 10
    Welche Töne? | Warum es funktioniert |
    Zur Harmonik | In Durtonarten 10
    Lead Sheet | Improvisierte Solos 12

2 **„A Minor Change"** 15
    Welche Töne? | Warum es funktioniert |
    Eine weitere Möglichkeit | Zur Harmonik |
    In Molltonarten 15
    Lead Sheet | Improvisierte Solos 17

3 **„The Key"** 20
    Welche Töne? | Warum es funktioniert |
    Zur Harmonik | In Durtonarten 20
    Lead Sheet | Improvisierte Solos 22

4 **„It's All Relative"** 25
    Welche Töne? | Warum es funktioniert |
    Eine weitere Möglichkeit | Zur Harmonik 25
    Lead Sheet | Improvisierte Solos 27

5 **„C Note"** 30
    Welche Töne? | Warum es funktioniert |
    Eine weitere Möglichkeit | Zur Harmonik |
    In Molltonarten 30
    Lead Sheet | Improvisierte Solos 32

6 **„Blue Riff"** 35
    Welche Töne? | Warum es funktioniert |
    Zur Harmonik 35
    Lead Sheet | Improvisierte Solos 38

7 **„Blue Funk"** 41
    Welche Töne? | Warum es funktioniert |
    Zur Harmonik 41
    Lead Sheet | Improvisierte Solos 43

8 **„Feelin' Blue"** 46
    Welche Töne? | Warum es funktioniert |
    Zur Harmonik 46
    Lead Sheet | Improvisierte Solos 48

9 "After the Spring" .... 51 What to Play | Why This Works | Other Options | About the Harmony............ 51 Lead Sheet | Improvised Solos 53	**9 „After the Spring"** .... 51 Welche Töne? | Warum es funktioniert | Weitere Möglichkeiten | Zur Harmonik.......... 51 Lead Sheet | Improvisierte Solos 53
10 Theory Guide.............................. 56 Key Signatures................................. 56 Scales... 56 Chords.. 58 II-V Progressions in Major Keys .... 60 II-V Progressions in Minor Keys 60	**10 Jazz-Theorie-Leitfaden** .... 56 Tonarten und Vorzeichen....................... 56 Tonleitern..................................... 56 Akkorde....................................... 58 II-V-Verbindungen in Durtonarten............... 60 II-V-Verbindungen in Molltonarten.............. 60
CD Track List	**CD Track List**

Improvising in Key Centers

One successful way to improvise is by using a *key-center-based approach*. In other words, if the music is in the key of B♭ major, notes from the B♭ major scale may be used for improvising. If the music in G minor, notes from G minor scale may be used. If the music has blues harmony, blues scales may be used. When improvisers use notes derived from these key centers, the notes "fit" and sound consonant and pleasing to the ear. Because the notes sound consonant, your confidence is boosted and you are then encouraged to go further with improvisation.

Most musicians–including those with limited experience playing jazz–are able to incorporate this key-center-based approach right away. It does not have a steep learning curve. A focus on key centers is particularly effective with developing improvisers.

The tunes in this book are presented in a *step-by-step sequence*–major keys first, then minor keys, then tunes with blues harmony. As you play through these tunes, you will gradually build confidence and improvisational skills so you can then master the music in this book.

Play-along recordings are included with the book so you can practice these concepts. Also included are recordings and transcriptions of improvised solos to help you with jazz phrasing and style ideas.

A Jazz Theory Guide is included that covers the theoretical principles used in this book.

Four Tips for New Improvisers

Play with confidence. *It is important to play jazz–and all music for that matter–with conviction.* Compel the audience to listen to you, mean what you say musically and project your ideas. Since improvising is making up music as you go along, you may not be sure of what you are about to play, but you must *play it as though you do know.*

Listen to jazz. It is impossible to play any kind of music without listening to it. There are certain qualities of jazz–tone quality, rhythmic interpretation, vibrato, phrasing–which can only be assimilated through careful listening. *Jazz musicians learn to play by copying what they hear on recordings.*

Improvisieren in tonalen Zentren

Ein Erfolg versprechender Ansatz ist das *Improvisieren in tonalen Zentren*. Mit anderen Worten: Wenn das Stück in B♭-Dur steht, können Töne der B♭-Durtonleiter zum Improvisieren verwendet werden. Steht das Stück in G-Moll, können Töne der G-Molltonleiter gespielt werden. Für Stücke mit Bluesakkorden können Bluestonleitern verwendet werden. Wenn beim Improvisieren Töne aus diesen tonalen Zentren verwendet werden, „passen" die Töne und klingen konsonant und angenehm fürs Ohr. Durch den angenehmen Klang der Töne wird dein Selbstvertrauen gestärkt, und du wirst motiviert, mit dem Improvisieren weiterzumachen.

Die meisten Musiker – auch Musiker, die nicht besonders viel von Jazz verstehen – können die Vorgabe, in tonalen Zentren zu improvisieren, sofort umsetzen. Die Methode ist leicht zu erlernen und insbesondere für Improvisationsneulinge ausgesprochen effektiv.

Die Stücke in diesem Buch bauen aufeinander auf: zuerst Durtonarten, dann Molltonarten, dann Stücke mit Bluesakkorden. Beim Spielen der Stücke bekommst du allmählich immer mehr Selbstvertrauen und erweiterst deine Improvisationskenntnisse, so dass du die Stücke in diesem Buch anschließend mühelos spielen kannst.

Das Buch enthält Playalong-Aufnahmen, damit du die Stücke üben kannst. Darüber hinaus sind Aufnahmen und Transkriptionen von improvisierten Solos enthalten, die dir Anregungen in Bezug auf Jazzphrasierung und Spieltechniken geben.

Ein Jazz-Theorie-Leitfaden ist ebenfalls enthalten. Er deckt die theoretischen Grundlagen ab, die in diesem Buch verwendet werden.

Vier Tipps für Improvisationsneulinge

Spiele selbstbewusst. *Es ist wichtig, Jazz – und auch jeden anderen Musikstil – mit Überzeugung zu spielen.* Du solltest das Publikum zwingen, dir zuzuhören, du solltest hinter deinen musikalischen Aussagen stehen, und du solltest deine Ideen vermitteln. Da du dir beim Improvisieren Musik ausdenkst, während du spielst, kann es zwar sein, dass du nicht sicher bist, was du spielen sollst, aber du musst es *immer so spielen, als wüsstest du es.*

Hör dir Jazzstücke an. Es ist unmöglich, Musik – egal welcher Stilrichtung – zu machen, ohne sie dir anzuhören. Jazz hat bestimmte Eigenschaften, z. B. Klangfarbe, rhythmische Interpretation, Vibrato, Phrasierung, die du dir nur durch intensives Zuhören zu eigen machen kannst. *Jazzmusiker lernen, indem sie nachspielen, was sie in Aufnahmen hören.*

Practice improvising. *The more you practice jazz, the better you will get at it.* Practice improvising in major keys, minor keys and with blues progressions. Practicing the tunes in this book will help you to build your improvisational skills.

Learn your scales and chords. It is not necessary to know a lot about music theory to start improvising. But as you progress as a jazz player, you will want to learn more about scales and chords. *Memorize scales and chords as they are introduced in this book.* Then, aspire to learn all you can about scales and chords.

About the Recordings

The Musicians

The following musicians are performing with the author, who is playing tenor saxophone.

Brian Ploeger, trumpet and flugelhorn
Brian is a *DownBeat* magazine award-winning musician who has toured the world and was a member of Maynard Ferguson's band.

Brian Ward, keyboards
Before joining the WSU faculty, Brian collaborated with Esperanza Spalding and Thara Memory in the creation of the Grammy Award-winning arrangement of Spalding's "City of Roses." He has also performed with Memory, Bobby Torres, Obo Addy, the Oregon Symphony and many others. Brian is Coordinator of Jazz Studies at Washington State University.

F. David Snider, bass
For over 20 years, Dave led groups in the U.S. Air Force and performed internationally. He has written over 500 compositions and arrangements and performed with Bobby Shew, Jon Faddis, Gabe Baltazar, Bill Watrous and Marvin Stamm. Dave is Instructor of Jazz Bass at Washington State University.

David Jarvis, drums
Dave has performed extensively as a jazz and classical percussionist. He is a widely published composer whose works are performed internationally. Dave is a Professor of Music at Washington State University.

Übe zu improvisieren. *Je mehr du übst, Jazz zu spielen, desto besser wirst du.* Übe in Durtonarten, Molltonarten und zu Blues-Akkordfolgen zu improvisieren. Wenn du die Stücke in diesem Buch übst, kannst du deine improvisatorischen Fähigkeiten ausbauen.

Lerne die Tonleitern und Akkorde. Man muss nicht viel über Musiktheorie wissen, um zu improvisieren. Doch wenn du als Jazzmusiker vorankommen willst, solltest du mehr über Tonleitern und Akkorde lernen. *Lerne die Tonleitern und Akkorde auswendig, die in diesem Buch vorgestellt werden.* Anschließend solltest du versuchen, so viel wie möglich über Tonleitern und Akkorde zu lernen.

Die Aufnahmen

Die Musiker

Die folgenden Musiker spielen mit dem Autor, der Tenorsaxophon spielt.

Brian Ploeger: Trompete und Flügelhorn
Brian Ploeger ist ein von der Zeitschrift *DownBeat* ausgezeichneter Musiker, der auf der ganzen Welt Konzerte gegeben hat und Mitglied in Maynard Fergusons Band war.

Brian Ward: Keyboards
Bevor er zur Washington State University kam, arbeitete Brian Ward mit Esperanza Spalding und Thara Memory an der Entstehung des Arrangements von Spaldings „City of Roses", das mit einem Grammy ausgezeichnet wurde. Darüber hinaus hat er u. a. mit Memory, Bobby Torres, Obo Addy und dem Oregon Symphony Orchestra gespielt. Ward ist Koordinator für das Jazzstudium an der Washington State University.

F. David Snider: Bass
David Snider ist seit über 20 Jahren Bandleader in der US Air Force und hatte schon viele internationale Auftritte. Er hat über 500 Kompositionen und Arrangements geschrieben und mit Bobby Shew, Jon Faddis, Gabe Baltazar, Bill Watrous und Marvin Stamm gespielt. Snider ist Dozent für Jazz-Bass an der Washington State University.

David Jarvis: Schlagzeug
Dave Jarvis ist ein erfahrener Jazz- und klassischer Perkussionist. Seine Kompositionen sind in zahlreichen Verlagen erschienen und werden weltweit gespielt. Jarvis ist Musikprofessor an der Washington State University.

Play-Along Recordings

On the play-along recordings, statements of the melody by the horns (trumpet or flugelhorn and tenor saxophone) alternate with rhythm section passages (piano, bass and drums) to provide accompaniment for your improvisations. When melodies return, you may play the melody with the horns, or you may continue to improvise.

Rhythm Section

On the play-along recordings, the keyboard is panned hard right and the bass is panned hard left. If you are a keyboard player, guitarist or bassist and wish to perform as an accompanist with the play-along recordings, you may adjust the stereo balance to eliminate the keyboard or bass while you are playing.

Improvised Solos

Improvised solos for each tune were recorded by the author on saxophone and Brian Ploeger on trumpet and flugelhorn. Their solos have been transcribed for you. The soloists moderated their improvising styles for these recordings. They avoided playing fast passages and mainly limited themselves to notes from the suggested scales and key centers in this book. Occasionally, some chromatic notes were included and notes were sometimes borrowed from parallel keys. *Parallel keys are those keys that share the same roots—C major is parallel to C minor and C Blues. Those chromatic notes and notes from parallel keys are indicated on the transcriptions.*

Try learning these improvised solos and playing them along with the recordings. This will help you develop jazz phrasing and style. You should also transcribe melodic ideas and solos from great jazz recordings. Transcription is one of the most important techniques utilized by accomplished jazz musicians as they learn to improvise.

Playalong-Aufnahmen

In den Playalongs wechseln sich Melodiepassagen der Bläser (Trompete oder Flügelhorn und Tenorsaxophon) mit Passagen der Rhythmusgruppe (Klavier, Bass und Schlagzeug) ab, um dich beim Improvisieren zu begleiten. Wenn die Melodie wiederkehrt, kannst du sie zusammen mit den Bläsern spielen oder aber weiter improvisieren.

Rhythmusgruppe

In den Playalongs ist das Keyboard ganz rechts und der Bass ganz links zu hören. Wenn du Keyboarder, Gitarrist oder Bassist bist und zu den Playalongs die Begleitung spielen willst, kannst du den Balanceregler an deiner Anlage so einstellen, dass Keyboard oder Bass nicht zu hören sind, wenn du spielst.

Improvisierte Solos

Für jedes Stück wurden vom Autor mit dem Saxophon und Brian Ploeger mit der Trompete und dem Flügelhorn improvisierte Solos eingespielt. Diese liegen hier als Transkriptionen vor. Die Solisten haben ihre Improvisationstechnik für die Aufnahmen gemäßigt. Sie haben schnelle Passagen vermieden und beschränken sich hauptsächlich auf Töne der Tonleitern und tonalen Zentren im Buch. Manchmal wurden ein paar chromatische Töne hinzugefügt oder Töne aus Varianttonarten verwendet. *Varianttonarten sind Tonarten mit demselben Grundton – C-Dur ist die Varianttonart von C-Moll und der C-Bluestonleiter. Die chromatischen Töne und Töne aus Varianttonarten sind in den Transkriptionen angegeben.*

Du solltest versuchen, die improvisierten Solos zu lernen und sie zu den Aufnahmen mitzuspielen. Dadurch kannst du die Jazzphrasierung und -technik besser erlernen. Außerdem solltest du Melodiekonzepte und Solos aus bekannten Jazzaufnahmen transkribieren. Transkribieren ist eine der wichtigsten Techniken, die versierte Jazzmusiker beim Improvisieren lernen angewandt haben.

1 "Getting Started"

What to Play

When playing "Getting Started," notes from the C major scale* may be used for improvisation throughout.

C major scale / C-Durtonleiter

Why This Works

"Getting Started" is composed in C major. C is the home base for the music and all of the notes in the melody and the chords are found in the C major scale. This is why when improvising, the notes from the key of C major–the notes in the C major scale–may be used throughout.

Learn to play the melody to "Getting Started" by playing with the play-along recording. The recording alternates between passages in which the melody is played and passages in which only the rhythm section instruments–piano, bass and drums–are playing. *It is during these rhythm section passages that you may improvise. When the melody returns, you may join in with the melodic statement or continue improvising.*

Become familiar with the notes in the C major scale. It is written out for you above and on the sheet music for "Getting Started." You may also play through the notes in the chords that are included on the music.

Once you are comfortable with the notes in C major, try improvising–making up your own melodies and rhythms–while playing with the recording.

It is not necessary to start on C when improvising using the notes from the C major scale. *You may start on any note you like and play in any register you want. You are not limited to one octave.* You may think of the notes in the C major scale as a collection of pitches, without a particular starting point or order. You may use any rhythms that you want.

Be sure to improvise with confidence. When playing with confidence, you will find that notes from the C major scale will sound good, or consonant, as you improvise.

---

* These musical terms are explained in the Jazz Theory Guide (p. 56).

1 „Getting Started"

Welche Töne?

Beim Improvisieren über „Getting Started" können durchgängig Noten der C-Durtonleiter* gespielt werden.

Warum es funktioniert

„Getting Started" steht in C-Dur. C ist die Tonart des Stücks, und alle Noten der Melodie und Akkorde sind in der C-Durtonleiter zu finden. Deshalb können beim Improvisieren durchgängig die Töne der Tonart C-Dur bzw. die Noten der C-Durtonleiter verwendet werden.

Du kannst die Melodie von „Getting Started" lernen, indem du zur Playalong-Aufnahme mitspielst. In der Aufnahme wird zwischen Passagen, in denen die Melodie gespielt wird und Passagen, in denen nur die Rhythmusgruppe – Klavier, Bass und Schlagzeug – spielt, abgewechselt. *Bei den Passagen mit der Rhythmusgruppe kannst du improvisieren. Wenn die Melodie wiederkehrt, kannst du entweder die Melodie mitspielen oder weiterhin improvisieren.*

Mach dich mit den Noten der C-Durtonleiter vertraut. Sie ist weiter oben sowie in den Noten zu „Getting Started" notiert. Du kannst auch die Töne der Akkorde spielen, die in den Noten angegeben sind.

Wenn du die Noten in C-Dur gut spielen kannst, probierst du zu improvisieren, d. h. dir eigene Melodien und Rhythmen auszudenken, während du zur Aufnahme mitspielst. *Du musst nicht mit C beginnen, wenn du mit den Tönen der C-Durtonleiter improvisierst, sondern kannst mit jedem beliebigen Ton anfangen und in jedem beliebigen Register spielen. Außerdem bist du nicht auf eine Oktave beschränkt.* Du kannst dir die Noten der C-Durtonleiter als Sammlung einzelner Töne vorstellen, die keinen bestimmten Anfangspunkt und keine Reihenfolge haben. Du kannst jeden beliebigen Rhythmus verwenden.

Improvisiere auf jeden Fall selbstbewusst. Wenn du selbstbewusst spielst, wirst du feststellen, dass die Töne der C-Durtonleiter beim Improvisieren gut bzw. konsonant klingen.

---

* Erklärungen zu diesen musikalischen Fachbegriffen findest du im Jazz-Theorie-Leitfaden (S. 56f.). Anm. zur deutschen Fassung: In der Jazz-, Rock- und Popmusik ist die internationale Schreibweise für Einzeltöne und Akkordsymbole üblich. Das deutsche „h" wird zu „B" bzw. „B♮", das deutsche „b" wird zu „B♭". „Fis", „cis" oder „as" werden mit Versetzungszeichen geschrieben: F♯, C♯ bzw. A♭.

About the Harmony

The chords for "Getting Started" provide the harmony for the tune. How these chords move and progress throughout the music is called the "chord progression." One time through a chord progression is called a "chorus."

There are three chords in "Getting Started" – Dm7, G7 and Cmaj7. The notes for all of these chords are from the C major scale.

- **Dm7** is built on the second step of the scale and is called a II chord (using the Roman numeral II).
- **G7** is built on the fifth step of the scale and is called a V chord.
- **Cmaj7** is built on the first step of the scale and is called a I chord.

This series of chords is called a II-V-I progression, one of the most common chord progressions in jazz.

Zur Harmonik

Die Akkorde zu „Getting Started" bilden die Harmonik des Stücks. Die Abfolge der Akkorde wird „Akkordverbindung" bzw. „Akkordfolge" genannt. Ein Durchgang durch die Akkordfolge eines ganzen Stücks wird als „Chorus" bezeichnet.

In „Getting Started" gibt es drei Akkorde: Dm7, G7 und Cmaj7. Die Töne aller Akkorde stammen aus der C-Dur-tonleiter.

- **Dm7** ist auf der zweiten Stufe der Tonleiter aufgebaut und heißt „Akkord auf der II. Stufe" (römische Ziffer II).
- **G7** ist auf der fünften Stufe der Tonleiter aufgebaut und heißt „Akkord auf der V. Stufe".
- **Cmaj7** ist auf der ersten Stufe der Tonleiter aufgebaut und heißt „Akkord auf der I. Stufe".

Diese Akkordabfolge wird als II-V-I-Verbindung bezeichnet und ist eine der häufigsten Akkordfolgen im Jazz.

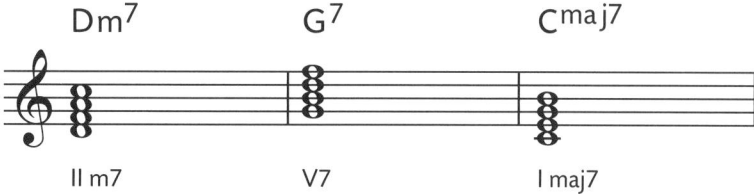

In Major Keys

- II chords are minor seventh chords.
- V chords are dominant seventh chords.
- I chords are major seventh chords.

In major keys also, II-V-I progressions are plain, without alterations.

In Durtonarten

- Der Akkord auf der II. Stufe ist ein kleiner Mollseptakkord.
- Der Akkord auf der V. Stufe ist ein Dominantseptakkord.
- Der Akkord auf der I. Stufe ist ein großer Durseptakkord (Major-7-Akkord).

In Durtonarten enthalten II-V-I-Verbindungen außerdem keine alterierten Töne.

Getting Started

Gregory W. Yasinitsky

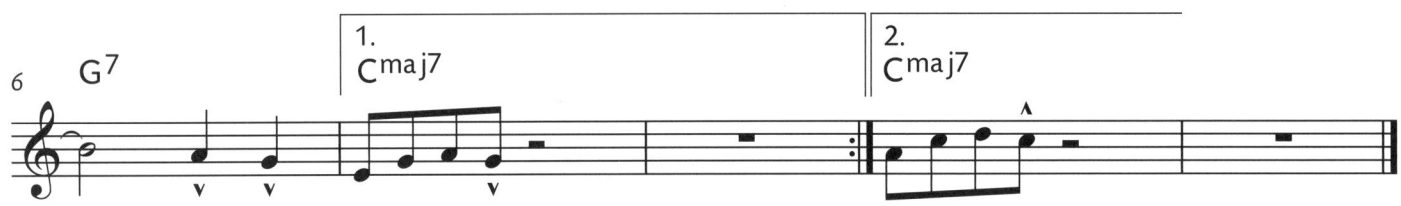

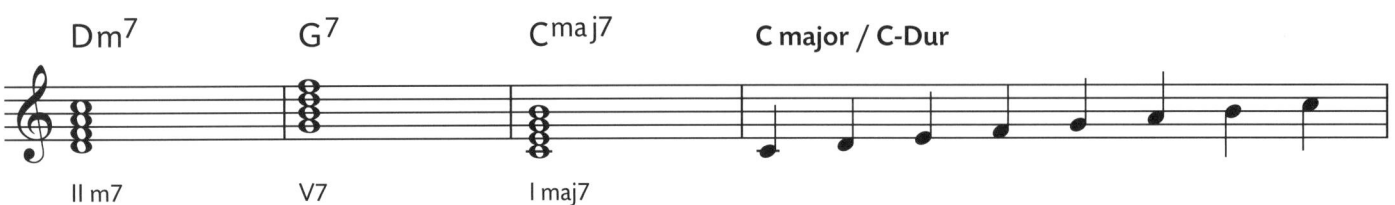

Getting Started – Tenor Saxophone Solo

Gregory W. Yasinitsky

© 2016 advance music GmbH, Mainz

Most of the notes in this solo are from the C major scale with a few chromatic notes used as grace notes.

Trumpet players may play all the tenor saxophone solos down an octave, if necessary.

Die meisten Noten in diesem Solo stammen aus der C-Dur-tonleiter, dazu gibt es einige chromatische Vorschlagsnoten.

Trompeter können alle Tenorsaxophonsolos eine Oktave tiefer spielen, wenn nötig.

Getting Started – Trumpet Solo

Brian Ploeger

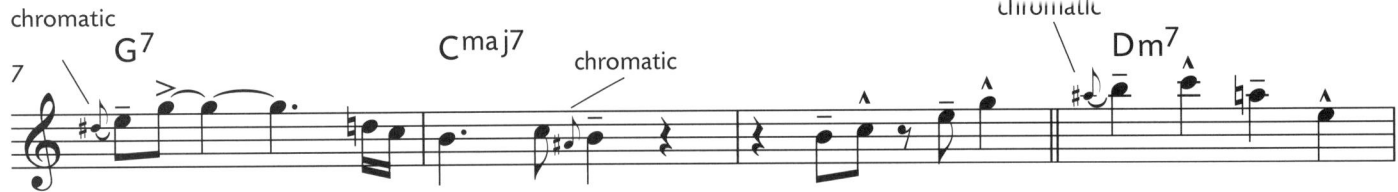
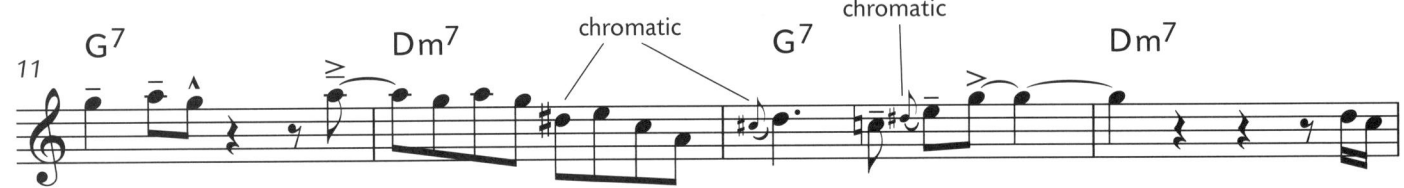

© 2016 advance music GmbH, Mainz

Most of the notes in this solo may be found in the C major scale except for a short passage from the C sweet blues scale (p. 35; parallel to C major) and some chromatic notes.

Die meisten Noten in diesem Solo stammen aus der C-Dur-tonleiter, mit Ausnahme einer kurzen Passage aus der „weichen" C-Bluestonleiter (s. S. 35; Varianttonleiter) und einigen chromatischen Vorschlägen.

2 "A Minor Change"

What to Play

When playing "A Minor Change," notes from the A natural minor scale may be used for improvisation throughout. These are the same notes in the C major scale that were used in "Getting Started."

used in *"A Minor Change"*
A natural minor

used in *"Getting Started"*
C major

Why This Works

"A Minor Change" is composed in A minor. A is the home base for the music and all of the notes in the melody and chords are in the key of A minor. This is why notes in the A natural minor scale work well for "A Minor Change."

The A natural minor scale has the same pitches found in the C major scale used for improvisation in the first tune in this collection, "Getting Started." *When keys share the same notes they are called "relative keys."* So, A minor and C major are relative keys.

Learn to play the melody to "A Minor Change" by playing with the play-along recording. The recording alternates between passages in which the melody is played, and passages in which only the rhythm section instruments–piano, bass and drums–are playing. *It is during these rhythm section passages that you may improvise. When the melody returns, you may join in with the melodic statement or continue improvising.*

Learn the A natural minor scale. Once you are comfortable with the notes, try improvising–making up your own melodies and rhythm while playing with the recording.

While improvising using notes from the A natural minor scale, it is not necessary to start on A. You may start on any note you and play in any register you want. You are not limited to one octave. Think of the notes in the scale as a collection of pitches, without a particular starting point or order. You may use any rhythms that you like. **Be sure to improvise with confidence.** When playing with confidence, you will find that notes from the A natural minor scale will *sound good, or consonant, as you improvise.*

Another Option

Another option for improvisation for "A Minor Change" is to use the notes in the A harmonic minor scale. There is a small difference between the A harmonic and A natural minor scales–there is a G♯ in the A harmonic minor scale and a G♮ in the A natural minor scale.

Eine weitere Möglichkeit

Eine weitere Möglichkeit, über „A Minor Change" zu improvisieren, ist, die Töne von A harmonisch Moll zu verwenden. Es gibt einen kleinen Unterschied zwischen den beiden A-Molltonleitern: A harmonisch Moll enthält ein G♯, A natürlich Moll ein G.

A harmonic minor / A harmonisch Moll

A natural minor / A natürlich Moll

Once you are comfortable with the notes in the A harmonic minor scale, try improvising–making up your own melodies and rhythms. You will hear that the A harmonic minor scale has a different sound than the A natural minor scale, but that the notes in both scales sound good.

Wenn du die Noten der harmonischen A-Molltonleiter gut spielen kannst, probierst du zu improvisieren, d. h. dir eigene Melodien und Rhythmen auszudenken. Du wirst hören, dass A harmonisch Moll zwar anders klingt als A natürlich Moll, die Töne aus beiden Tonleitern jedoch gut klingen.

About the Harmony

There are three chords in "A Minor Change." The notes for these chords are found in the key of A minor.

- **Bm7(♭5)** is a II chord built on the second step of the key.
- **E7(♭9)** is a V chord built on the fifth step of the key.
- **Am** is a I chord built on the first step of the key.

This series of chords is a II-V-I progression.

Zur Harmonik

„A Minor Change" enthält drei Akkorde. Die Töne der Akkorde sind in der Tonart A-Moll zu finden.

- **Bm7(♭5)** ist ein Akkord auf der II. Stufe der Tonleiter.
- **E7(♭9)** ist ein Akkord auf der V. Stufe der Tonleiter.
- **Am** ist ein Akkord auf der I. Stufe der Tonleiter.

Die Abfolge der Akkorde bildet wiederum eine II-V-I-Verbindung.

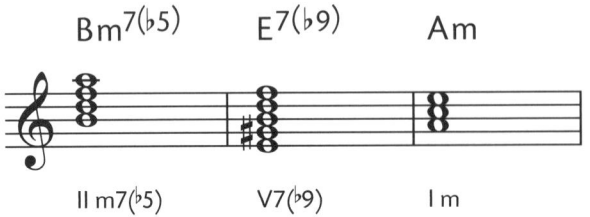

In Minor Keys

- II chords are minor seventh flat five chords (sometimes called half-diminished chords).
- V chords are dominant seventh chords with flat nines.
- I chords are minor chords.

In minor keys, II-V-I progressions are "altered," with alterations on the II and V chords. These alterations can make the progression look complicated, but they simply mean that the progression is in a minor key.

In Molltonarten

- Der Akkord auf der II. Stufe ist ein kleiner Mollseptakkord mit verminderter Quinte (auch halbverminderter Septakkord genannt).
- Der Akkord auf der V. Stufe ist ein Dominantseptakkord mit kleiner None.
- Der Akkord auf der I. Stufe ist ein Mollakkord.

Bei den II-V-I-Verbindungen in Molltonarten enthalten die Akkorde auf der II. und V. Stufe alterierte Töne. Dadurch sehen die Akkordfolgen zwar kompliziert aus, doch bedeuten die Alternationen lediglich, dass es sich um eine Akkordfolge in einer Molltonart handelt.

A Minor Change

Gregory W. Yasinitsky

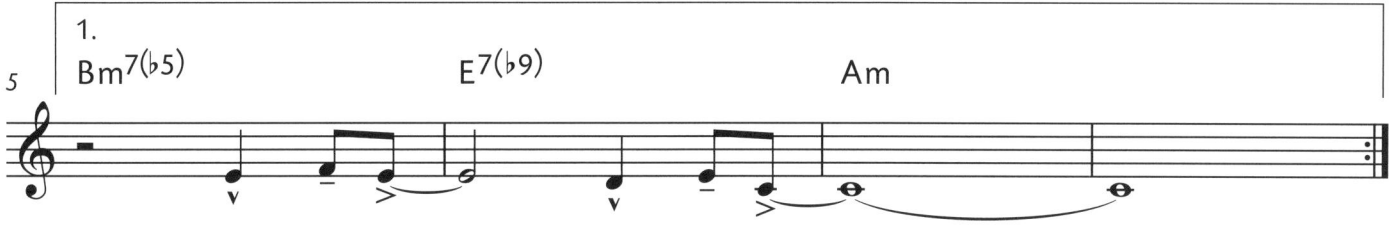
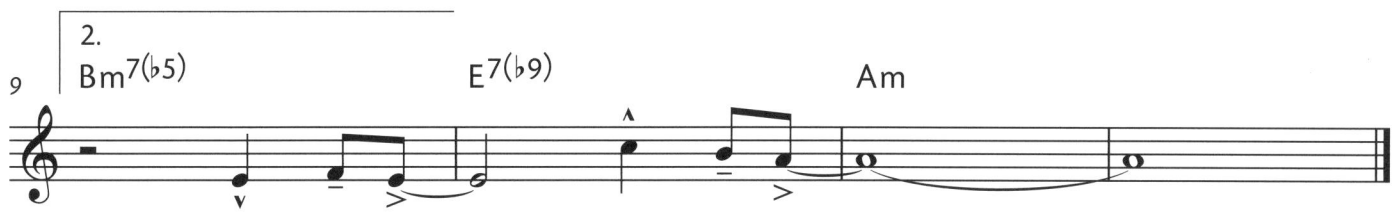

© 2016 advance music GmbH, Mainz

Tenor saxophonists should play this tune up an octave.

Tenorsaxophonisten sollten diese Melodie eine Oktave höher spielen.

A Minor Change – Tenor Saxophone Solo

Gregory W. Yasinitsky

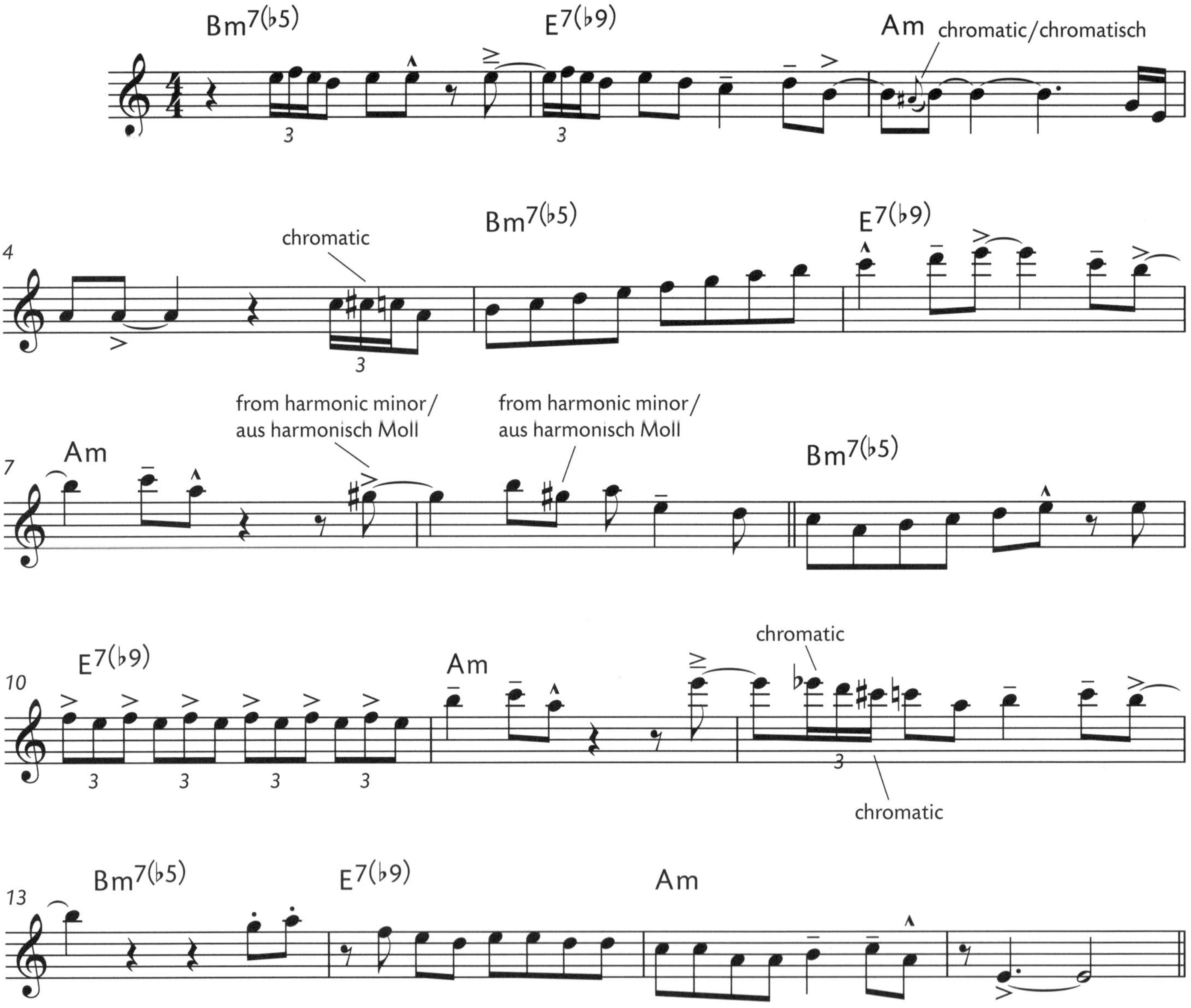

Most of the notes in this solo are from the A natural minor and A harmonic minor scales with a few chromatic approach notes or passing tones here and there.

Die meisten Noten in diesem Solo stammen aus A natürlich bzw. harmonisch Moll, dazu gibt es einige chromatische Vorschläge oder Durchgangstöne.

A Minor Change – Flugelhorn Solo

Brian Ploeger

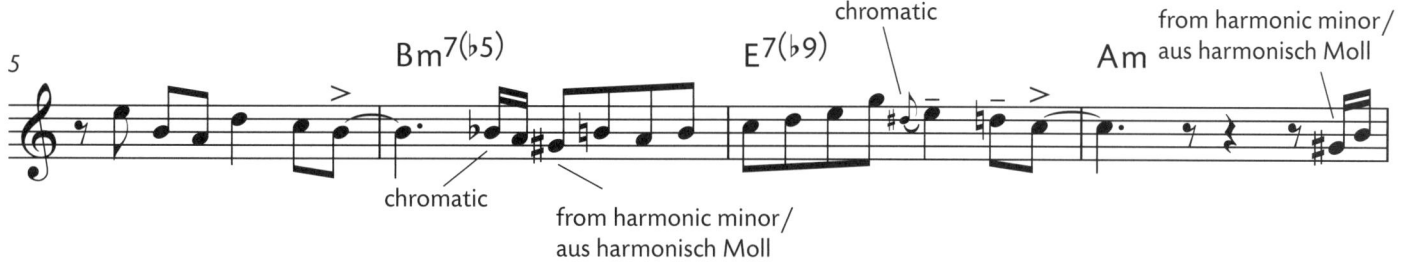

© 2016 advance music GmbH, Mainz

Most of the notes in this solo may be found in the A natural minor and A harmonic minor scales except for some chromatic approach notes or passing tones here and there.

Die meisten Noten in diesem Solo stammen aus A natürlich bzw. harmonisch Moll, mit Ausnahme einiger chromatischer Vorschläge oder Durchgangstönen.

3 "The Key"

What to Play

When playing "The Key," notes from the G major scale may be used for improvisation throughout.

G major / G-Dur

Why This Works

"The Key" is composed in G major. The note G is the home base for the music and all of the notes used the melody and chords may be found in the key of G major. This is why the notes in the G major scale work well for "The Key". The G major scale has only one note that is different from the notes found in the C major scale (the notes used in "Getting Started," the first tune in this book) and in the A natural minor scale (used in "A Minor Change," the second tune in this book). There is an F♯ in the G major scale and an F♮ in the C major and A natural minor scales.

Learn to play the melody to "The Key" by playing with the play-along recording. The recording alternates between passages when the melody is played, and passages when only the rhythm section instruments–piano, bass and drums–are played. *It is during these rhythm section passages that you may improvise. When the melody returns, you may join in with the melodic statement or continue improvising.*

Become familiar with the notes in the G major scale. It is written out for you on the sheet music for "The Key." You may also play through the notes in the chords included on the music. Once you are comfortable with the notes in G major, try improvising–making up your own melodies and rhythms–while playing with the recording.

When improvising with the notes from the G major scale, it is not necessary to start on G. You may start on any note you want and play in any register you want. You are not limited to one octave. Think of the notes in the G major scale as a collection of pitches, without a particular starting point or order. You may also use any rhythms you want. **Be sure to**

improvise with confidence. When playing with confidence, you will find that notes from G major will sound good, or consonant, as you improvise.

About the Harmony

There are three chords in "The Key." The notes for all of these chords are found in the G major scale.

- **Am7** is built on the second step of the scale and is called a II chord.
- **D7** is built on the fifth step of the scale and is called a V chord.
- **Gmaj7** is built on the first step of the scale and is called a I chord.

This series of chords is called a *II-V-I progression, one of the most common chord progressions in jazz.*

In Major Keys

- II chords are minor seventh chords.
- V chords are dominant seventh chords.
- I chords are major seventh chords.

Stell dir die Noten der G-Durtonleiter als Sammlung einzelner Töne vor, die keinen bestimmten Anfangspunkt und keine Reihenfolge haben. Du kannst auch jeden beliebigen Rhythmus verwenden. **Improvisiere auf jeden Fall selbstbewusst.** Wenn du selbstbewusst spielst, wirst du feststellen, dass die Töne der G-Durtonleiter beim Improvisieren gut bzw. konsonant klingen.

Zur Harmonik

„The Key" enthält drei Akkorde. Die Töne aller Akkorde kommen in der G-Durtonleiter vor.

- **Am7** ist ein Akkord auf der II. Stufe der Tonleiter.
- **D7** ist ein Akkord auf der V. Stufe der Tonleiter.
- **Gmaj7** ist ein Akkord auf der I. Stufe der Tonleiter.

Diese Akkordfolge wird als *II-V-I-Verbindung* bezeichnet und *ist eine der häufigsten Akkordfolgen im Jazz.*

In Durtonarten

- Der Akkord auf der II. Stufe ist ein kleiner Mollseptakkord.
- Der Akkord auf der V. Stufe ist ein Dominantseptakkord.
- Der Akkord auf der I. Stufe ist ein großer Durseptakkord (Major-7-Akkord).

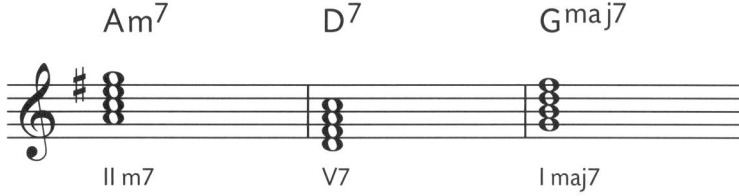

In major keys, II-V-I progressions are "plain," without alterations.

In Durtonarten enthalten II-V-I-Verbindungen keine alterierten Töne.

The Key

Gregory W. Yasinitsky

The Key – Tenor Saxophone Solo

Gregory W. Yasinitsky

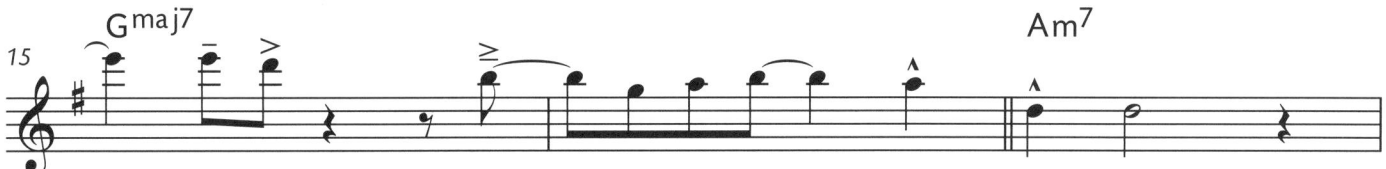

© 2016 advance music GmbH, Mainz

All the notes in this solo are from the G major scale.

Alle Noten in diesem Solo stammen aus der G-Durtonleiter.

The Key – Trumpet Solo

Brian Ploeger

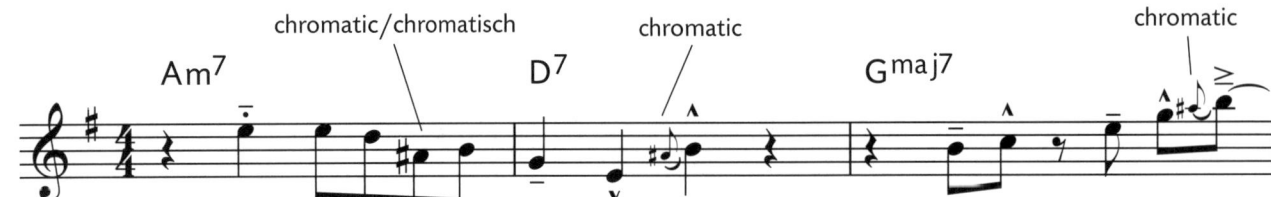

© 2016 advance music GmbH, Mainz

Most of the notes in this solo may be found in the G major scale with some chromatic passing tones or approach notes here and there.

Die meisten Noten in diesem Solo stammen aus der G-Dur-tonleiter, dazu gibt es einige chromatische Vorschläge oder Durchgangsnoten.

4 "It's All Relative"

What to Play

When playing "It's All Relative," notes from the E natural minor and G major scales may be used for improvisation throughout. These two scales share the same notes because they are from relative keys—E minor and G major. *Relative keys are keys that share the same notes.*

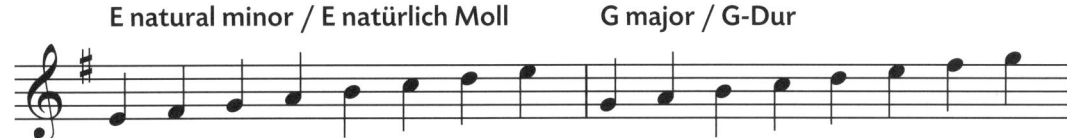

E natural minor | G major

Why This Works

"It's All Relative" is composed in the relative keys of E minor and G major. *Relative keys are those that start on different roots, but share the same key signature.* The key signature for E minor has one sharp (F♯) as does the key of G major, so E minor and G major are relative keys.

The first eight bars of "It's All Relative" are in E minor, with E as the home base, and the second eight bars are in G major, with G as the home base. This is why the notes from the E natural minor and G major scales may be used for improvisation throughout.

Learn to play the melody to "It's All Relative" by playing the melody with the play-along recording. The recording alternates between passages in which the melody is played, and passages in which only the rhythm section instruments–piano, bass and drums–are played. *It is during these rhythm section passages that you may improvise. When the melody returns, you may join in with the melodic statement or continue improvising.*

Become familiar with the notes in the E natural minor and G major scales and the chords for "It's All Relative." They are written out on the sheet music. Once you are comfortable with the notes in E minor and G major, try improvising–making up your own melodies and rhythms.

When improvising using the notes from E natural minor, it is not necessary to start on E, and when improvising using the notes in G major, it is not necessary to start on G. You may start on any note you want and play in any register you want. You are not limited to one octave.

It is useful to think of the notes in these relative keys–E minor and G major–as a collection of pitches, without a particular starting point or order. You may use any rhythms you like. **Be sure to improvise with confidence.**

Another Option

In the E minor section of the tune, the first eight bars, you may also use notes from the E harmonic minor scale which has only one note that is different from the notes in the E natural minor scale. In E harmonic minor there is a D♯ and in E natural minor there is a D♮.

Eine weitere Möglichkeit

Im E-Moll-Teil des Stücks, den ersten acht Takten, kannst du auch Töne aus E harmonisch Moll verwenden, die sich in nur einem Ton von E natürlich Moll unterscheidet: E harmonisch Moll enthält ein D♯, E natürlich Moll ein D.

About the Harmony

There are three chords in the E minor section of "It's All Relative."

- **F♯m7(♭5)** is a II chord built on the second step of E minor.
- **B7(♭9)** is a V chord built on the fifth step of E minor.
- **Em** is a I chord built on the first step of E minor.

This is a II-V-I progression in E minor. *We know that this is a II-V-I in a minor key because the II and V chords have alterations.*

There are three chords in the G major section of the tune.

- **Am7** is a II chord built on the second step of G major.
- **D7** is a V chord built on the fifth step of G major.
- **Gmaj7** is a I chord built on the first step of G major.

This is a II-V-I progression in G major. *We know that this is a II-V-I in a major key because the II and V chords are plain, without alterations.*

Zur Harmonik

Der E-Moll-Teil von „It's All Relative" enthält drei Akkorde.

- **F♯m7(♭5)** ist ein Akkord auf der II. Stufe von E-Moll.
- **B7(♭9)** ist ein Akkord auf der V. Stufe von E-Moll.
- **Em** ist ein Akkord auf der I. Stufe von E-Moll.

Dies ist eine II-V-I-Verbindung in E-Moll. *Wir wissen, dass es sich um eine II-V-I-Akkordfolge in einer Molltonart handelt, da die Akkorde auf der II. und V. Stufe alterierte Töne enthalten.*

Der G-Dur-Teil von „It's All Relative" enthält drei Akkorde.

- **Am7** ist ein Akkord auf der II. Stufe von G-Dur.
- **D7** ist ein Akkord auf der V. Stufe von G-Dur.
- **Gmaj7** ist ein Akkord auf der I. Stufe von G-Dur.

Dies ist eine II-V-I-Verbindung in G-Dur. *Wir wissen, dass es sich um eine II-V-I-Verbindung in einer Durtonart handelt, da die Akkorde auf der II. und V. Stufe keine alterierte Töne enthalten.*

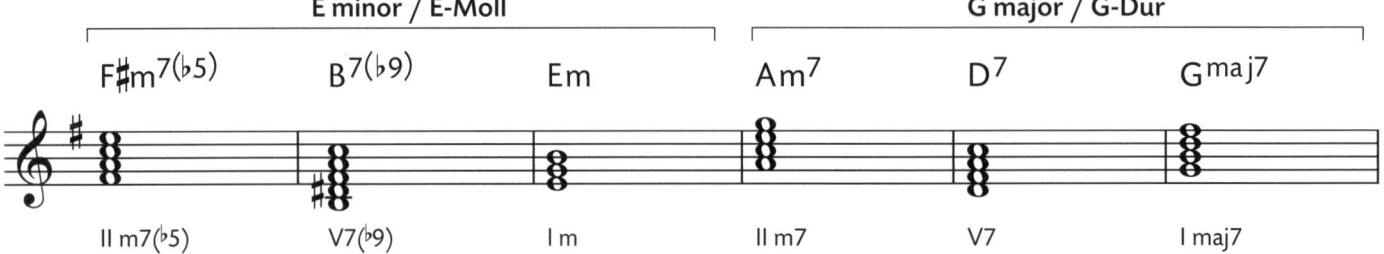

It's All Relative

Gregory W. Yasinitsky

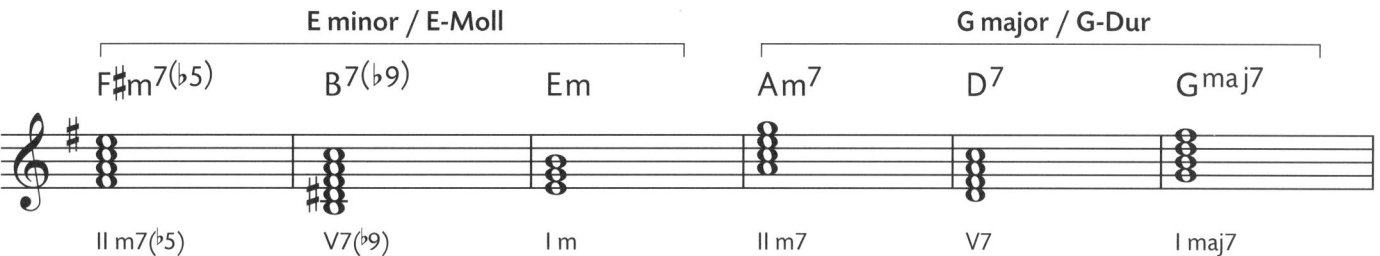

© 2016 advance music GmbH, Mainz

It's All Relative – Tenor Saxophone Solo

Gregory W. Yasinitsky

© 2016 advance music GmbH, Mainz

Most of the notes in this solo are from the E natural minor, E harmonic minor and G major scales with a few chromatic notes used here and there.

Die meisten Noten in diesem Solo stammen aus E natürlich bzw. harmonisch Moll sowie G-Dur, dazu gibt es einige chromatische Töne.

It's All Relative – Flugelhorn Solo

Brian Ploeger

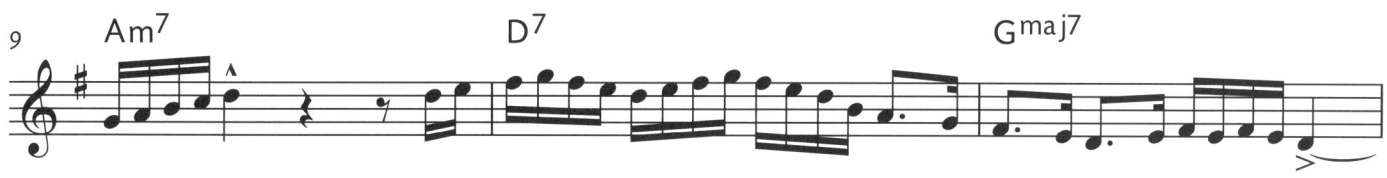

© 2016 advance music GmbH, Mainz

Most of the notes in this solo may be found in the E natural minor and G major scales.

Die meisten Noten in diesem Solo stammen aus E natürlich Moll und G-Dur.

5 "C Note"

What to Play

When playing "C Note," notes from the D natural minor scale may be used for improvisation throughout. These are the same notes found in the F major scale.

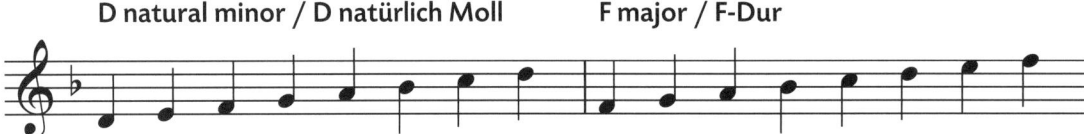

D natural minor / D natürlich Moll   F major / F-Dur

Why This Works

"C Note" is composed in D minor. D is the home base for the music and all of the notes in the melody and chords may be found the key of D minor. This is why notes from the D natural minor scale work well throughout. If you are more familiar with major scales, you may think of the D natural minor scale as an F major scale starting on D. This is because D minor and F major are relative keys. *Relative keys share the same key signature and therefore the same notes.*

Learn to play the melody to "C Note" by playing with the play-along recording. The recording alternates between passages when the melody is played, and passages when only the rhythm section instruments–piano, bass and drums–are played. *It is during these rhythm section passages that you may improvise. When the melody returns, you may join in with the melodic statement or continue improvising.*

Learn the D natural minor scale. Once you are comfortable with the notes, try improvising–making up your own melodies and rhythms.

While improvising using notes from the D natural minor scale, it is not necessary to start on D. You may start on any note you want and play in any register you want. You are not limited to one octave. Think of the notes of the scale as a collection of pitches, without a particular starting point or order. You may use any rhythms that you like. **Be sure to improvise with confidence.**

Another Option

Another option for improvisation for "C Note" is to use the notes from the D harmonic minor scale (also provided on your music). There is a small difference between the D harmonic and D natural minor scales–there is a C♯ in the D harmonic minor scale and a C♮ in the D natural minor scale.

---

5 „C Note"

Welche Töne?

Beim Improvisieren über „C Note" können durchgängig Töne aus D natürlich Moll gespielt werden. Es sind dieselben Noten wie die der F-Durtonleiter.

Warum es funktioniert

„C Note" steht in D-Moll. D ist der Grundton des Stücks, und alle Noten der Melodie und Akkorde sind in der D-Molltonleiter enthalten. Deshalb funktionieren die Töne der D-Molltonleiter beim Improvisieren zu „C Note" durchgängig gut. Wenn du eher mit den Durtonleitern vertraut bist, kannst du dir D natürlich Moll als F-Durtonleiter vorstellen, die mit D beginnt – weil D-Moll und F-Dur Paralleltonarten sind. *Paralleltonarten sind Tonarten, die dieselben Töne enthalten.*

Du kannst die Melodie von „C Note" lernen, indem du zur Playalong-Aufnahme mitspielst. In der Aufnahme wird zwischen Passagen, in denen die Melodie gespielt wird und Passagen, in denen nur die Rhythmusgruppe – Klavier, Bass und Schlagzeug – spielt, abgewechselt. *Bei den Passagen mit der Rhythmusgruppe kannst du improvisieren. Wenn die Melodie wiederkehrt, kannst du entweder die Melodie mitspielen oder weiterhin improvisieren.*

Lerne die Tonleiter D natürlich Moll. Wenn du sie gut spielen kannst, probierst du zu improvisieren, d. h. dir eigene Melodien und Rhythmen auszudenken.

Du musst nicht mit D beginnen, wenn du mit den Tönen von D natürlich Moll improvisierst, sondern kannst mit jedem beliebigen Ton anfangen und in jedem beliebigen Register spielen. Außerdem bist du nicht auf eine Oktave beschränkt. Stell dir die Töne der D-Molltonleiter als Sammlung einzelner Töne vor, die keinen bestimmten Anfangspunkt und keine Reihenfolge haben. Du kannst jeden beliebigen Rhythmus verwenden. **Improvisiere auf jeden Fall selbstbewusst.**

Eine weitere Möglichkeit

Eine weitere Möglichkeit, über „C Note" zu improvisieren, ist, die Töne von D harmonisch Moll zu verwenden (die ebenfalls in den Noten angegeben sind). Es gibt einen kleinen Unterschied zwischen den beiden D-Molltonleitern: D harmonisch Moll enthält ein C♯ und D natürlich Moll ein C♮.

Once you are comfortable with the notes in the D harmonic minor scale, try improvising–making up your own melodies and rhythms. You will hear that the D harmonic minor scale has a different sound than the D natural minor scale, but that the notes in both scales sound good.

About the Harmony

There are three chords in "C Note."

- **Em7(♭5)** is a II chord built on the second step of the key.
- **A7(♭9)** is a V chord built on the fifth step of the key.
- **Dm** is a I chord built on the first step of the key.

This series of chords is a II-V-I progression.

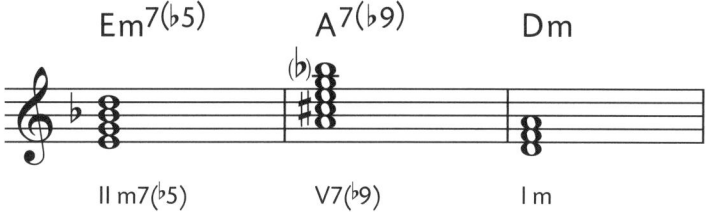

In Minor Keys

- II chords are minor seventh flat five chords.
- V chords are dominant seventh chords with flat nines.
- I chords are minor chords.

In minor keys, II-V-I progressions have alterations on the II and V chords. These alterations can make the progression look complicated, but they simply mean that the progression is in a minor key.

Zur Harmonik

„C Note" enthält drei Akkorde.

- **Em7(♭5)** ist ein Akkord auf der II. Stufe der Tonleiter.
- **A7(♭9)** ist ein Akkord auf der V. Stufe der Tonleiter.
- **Dm** ist ein Akkord auf der I. Stufe der Tonleiter.

Diese Akkordfolge ist eine II-V-I-Verbindung.

In Molltonarten

- Der Akkord auf der II. Stufe ist ein kleiner Mollseptakkord mit verminderter Quinte (auch halbverminderter Septakkord genannt).
- Der Akkord auf der V. Stufe ist ein Dominantseptakkord mit kleiner None.
- Der Akkord auf der I. Stufe ist ein Mollakkord.

Bei den II-V-I-Verbindungen in Molltonarten enthalten die Akkorde auf der II. und V. Stufe alterierte Töne. Dadurch sehen die Akkordfolgen zwar kompliziert aus, doch bedeuten die Alternationen lediglich, dass es sich um eine Akkordfolge in einer Molltonart handelt.

C Note

Gregory W. Yasinitsky

15

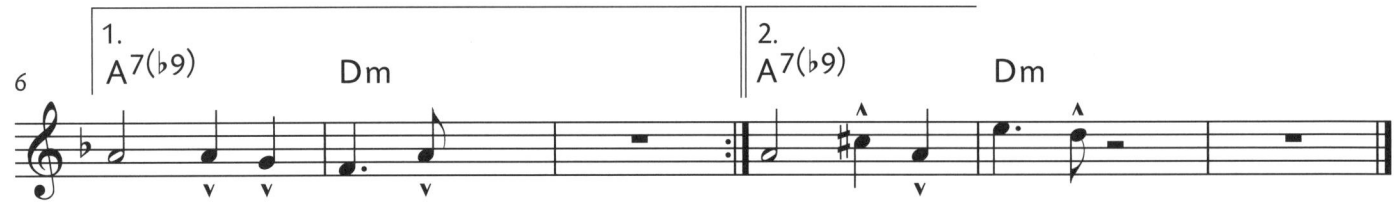

© 2016 advance music GmbH, Mainz

C Note – Tenor Saxophone Solo

Gregory W. Yasinitsky

Most of the notes in this solo are from the D natural minor and D harmonic minor scales with a few chromatic notes added here and there.

Die meisten Noten in diesem Solo sind aus D natürlich bzw. harmonisch Moll, dazu einige chromatische Töne.

© 2016 advance music GmbH, Mainz

C Note – Trumpet Solo

Brian Ploeger

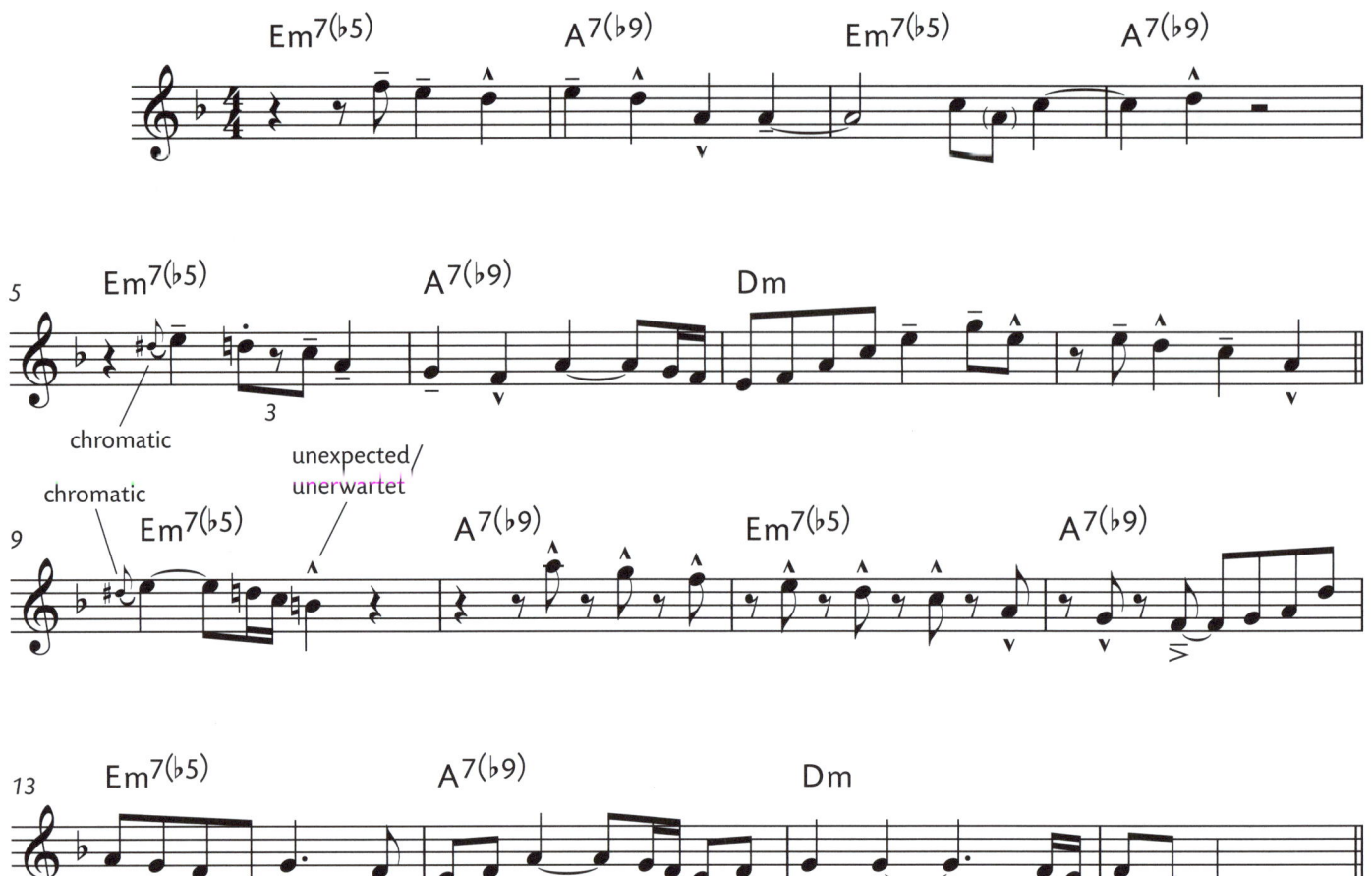

© 2016 advance music GmbH, Mainz

Most of the notes in this solo may be found in the D natural minor scale with a couple of chromatic approaches and an unexpected B natural.

Die meisten Noten in diesem Solo stammen aus D natürlich Moll, dazu gibt es einige chromatische Annäherungstöne und ein unerwartetes B (H).

6 "Blue Riff"

What to Play

When playing "Blue Riff," notes from the C "standard" blues scale and C "sweet" blues scale* may be used for improvisation throughout.

To begin with, you may wish to limit yourself to notes from one of these blues scales when improvising on "Blue Riff." As you become more experienced, you may alternate between the two blues scales whenever and wherever you like. *Combining these two scales into one composite scale does not work well, though.*

Why This Works

"Blue Riff" is a blues tune composed in C. It is constructed from a "riff," a short, four-measure idea, which is repeated three times. Because "Blue Riff" is a blues tune, blues scales may be used for improvisation throughout.

On the music, there is a set of notes labeled as the "standard" blues scale. This is the blues scale most commonly taught.

It is constructed as follows – 1 • b3 • 4 • #4 • 5 • b7. *This standard blues scale sounds good against the entire chord progression.*

There is another blues scale often used by jazz musicians for improvisation. *This scale is included on the music and is labeled the "sweet" blues scale.* It is constructed as follows – 1 • 2 • b3 • ♮3 • 5 • 6.

---

* "Sweet" refers to the mellow sound of this scale when compared to the harsh and more dissonant sound of the standard blues scale.

The C sweet blues scale has the same notes as the A standard blues scale, but starts on C.

Die „weiche" C-Bluestonleiter enthält dieselben Töne wie die A-Bluestonleiter, beginnt jedoch mit C.

Like the C standard blues scale, the C sweet blues scale works well throughout the chord progression. When using the sweet blues scale, be careful of using E♮ against the F7 chords. The E will clash with the E♭, the seventh of the F7 chord. So, playing E♭ against the F7 chords will be a better choice.

Learn to play the melody to "Blue Riff" by playing with the play-along recording. The recording alternates between passages in which the melody is played and passages in which only the rhythm section instruments–piano, bass and drums–are playing. *It is during these rhythm section passages that you may improvise. When the melody returns, you may join in with the melodic statement or continue improvising.*

Become familiar with the notes in both the standard and sweet blues scales. Once you are comfortable with the notes in these scales, try improvising – making up your own melodies and rhythms. **Be sure to improvise with confidence.**

When using these C blues scales to improvise, it is not necessary to start on C. You may start on any note you want and play in any register you want. You are not limited to one octave. Think of the notes in each scale as a set of pitches that may be played without a particular starting point or order.

You may alternate between these two blues scales whenever and wherever you like. *Combining these two scales into one composite scale does not work well, though.*

There are unique expressive devices used by the best blues improvisers–scoops, bends, slurs and more. You should listen to great soloists using blues ideas to emulate the phrasing and inflections used by these accomplished jazz artists.

About the Harmony

Blues has a unique harmonic structure, different from major and minor key harmony. There are many harmonic variations of blues. The most common form is twelve bars long and is referred to as a "twelve-bar blues."

Blues progressions generally include dominant seventh chords built on the first, fourth and fifth steps of the key (I, IV and V). Also, in jazz, a blues progression will typically include a II-V progression in bars 9 and 10. These harmon-

Wie die C-Bluestonleiter klingt auch die „weiche" C-Bluestonleiter über die gesamte Akkordfolge gut. Wenn du die weiche Bluestonleiter verwendest, solltest du aufpassen, wenn du ein E zum F7-Akkord spielst. Das E kollidiert mit dem E♭, der Septime des F7-Akkords. Daher ist es besser, ein E♭ zum F7-Akkord zu spielen.

Du kannst die Melodie von „Blue Riff" lernen, indem du zur Playalong-Aufnahme mitspielst. In der Aufnahme wird zwischen Passagen, in denen die Melodie gespielt wird und Passagen, in denen nur die Rhythmusgruppe – Klavier, Bass und Schlagzeug – spielt, abgewechselt. *Bei den Passagen mit der Rhythmusgruppe kannst du improvisieren. Wenn die Melodie wiederkehrt, kannst du entweder die Melodie mitspielen oder weiterhin improvisieren.*

Lerne sowohl die Bluestonleiter als auch die weiche Bluestonleiter. Wenn du die Noten in beiden Tonleitern gut spielen kannst, probierst du zu improvisieren, d. h. dir eigene Melodien und Rhythmen auszudenken. **Improvisiere auf jeden Fall selbstbewusst.**

Du musst nicht mit C beginnen, wenn du mit den Tönen der C-Bluestonleitern improvisierst, sondern kannst mit jedem beliebigen Ton anfangen und in jedem beliebigen Register spielen. Außerdem bist du nicht auf eine Oktave beschränkt. Stell dir die Töne der jeweiligen Tonleiter als Sammlung einzelner Töne vor, die keinen bestimmten Anfangspunkt und keine Reihenfolge haben.

Du kannst zwischen den beiden Bluestonleitern abwechseln, wann und wo immer du willst. *Allerdings funktioniert es nicht gut, die beiden Tonleitern zu einer zusammengesetzten Tonleiter zu kombinieren.*

Es gibt viele Spieltechniken, die von den besten Bluesmusikern beim Improvisieren verwendet werden: Scoop, Bending, Slur etc. Hör dir bekannte Solisten an, die Bluesmotive spielen, um die Phrasierung und Verzierungen dieser versierten Jazzmusiker nachzuahmen.

Zur Harmonik

Bluesstücke haben eine spezielle Harmonik, die sich von der Harmonik in Dur- und Molltonarten unterscheidet. Außerdem gibt es viele harmonische Variationen. Die geläufigste Blues-Form besteht aus zwölf Takten und wird als „zwölftaktiger Blues" bezeichnet.

Blues-Akkordverbindungen enthalten üblicherweise Dominantseptakkorde auf der I., IV. und V. Stufe der Tonleiter. Im Jazz enthält eine Blues-Akkordfolge außerdem in Takt 9

ic features may be found in the chord progression for "Blue Riff."

Study the chord progression and structure of "Blue Riff." *Work to memorize the progression.* Accomplished jazz musicians are expected to know how to construct typical blues progressions.

und 10 eine II-V-Verbindung. Diese harmonischen Eigenschaften sind in der Akkordfolge zu „Blue Riff" zu finden.

Sieh dir die Akkordfolge und den Aufbau von „Blue Riff" genau an. *Präge dir die Akkordverbindung gut ein.* Von versierten Jazzmusikern wird erwartet, dass sie typische Blues-Akkordverbindungen spielen können.

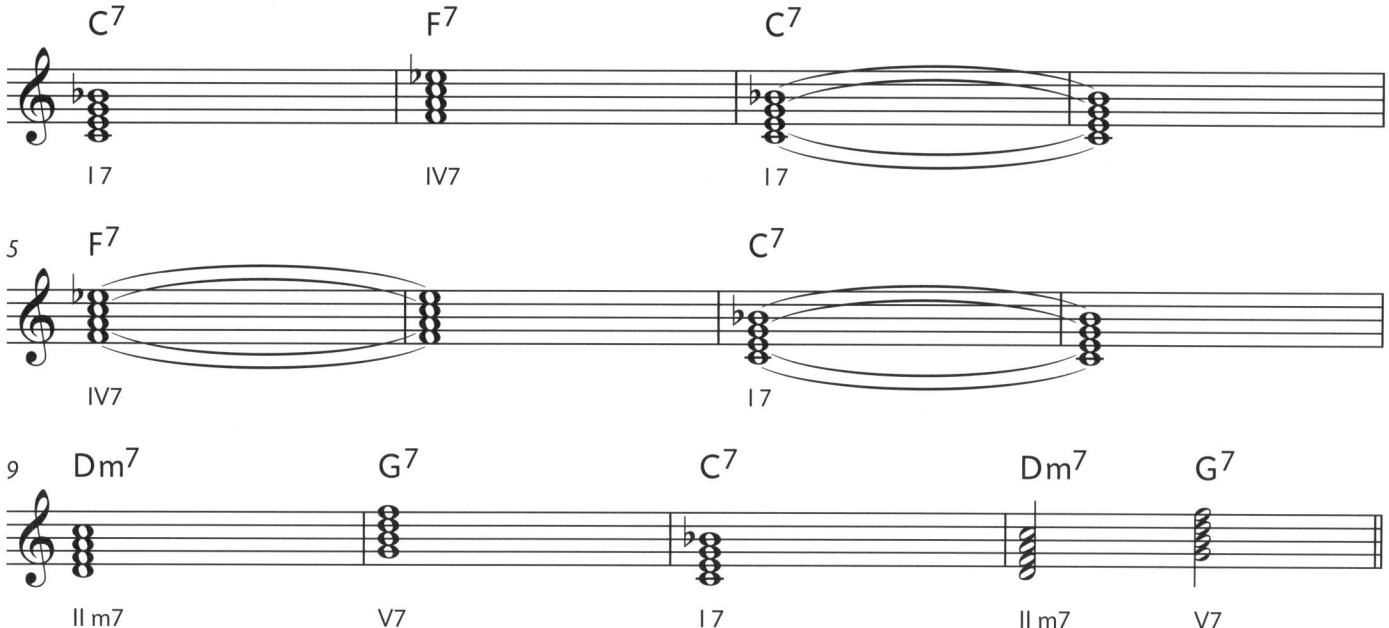

Blue Riff

Gregory W. Yasinitsky

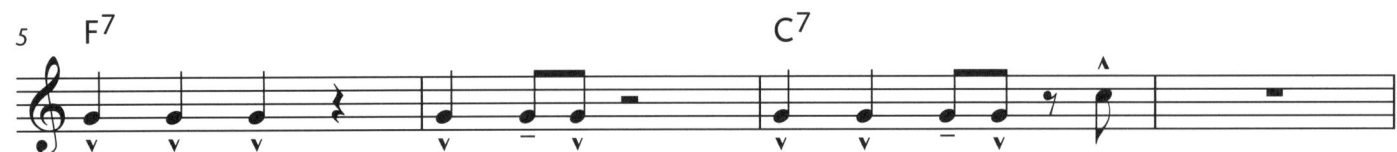
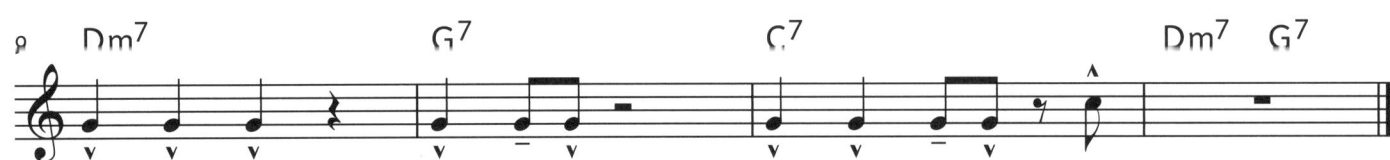
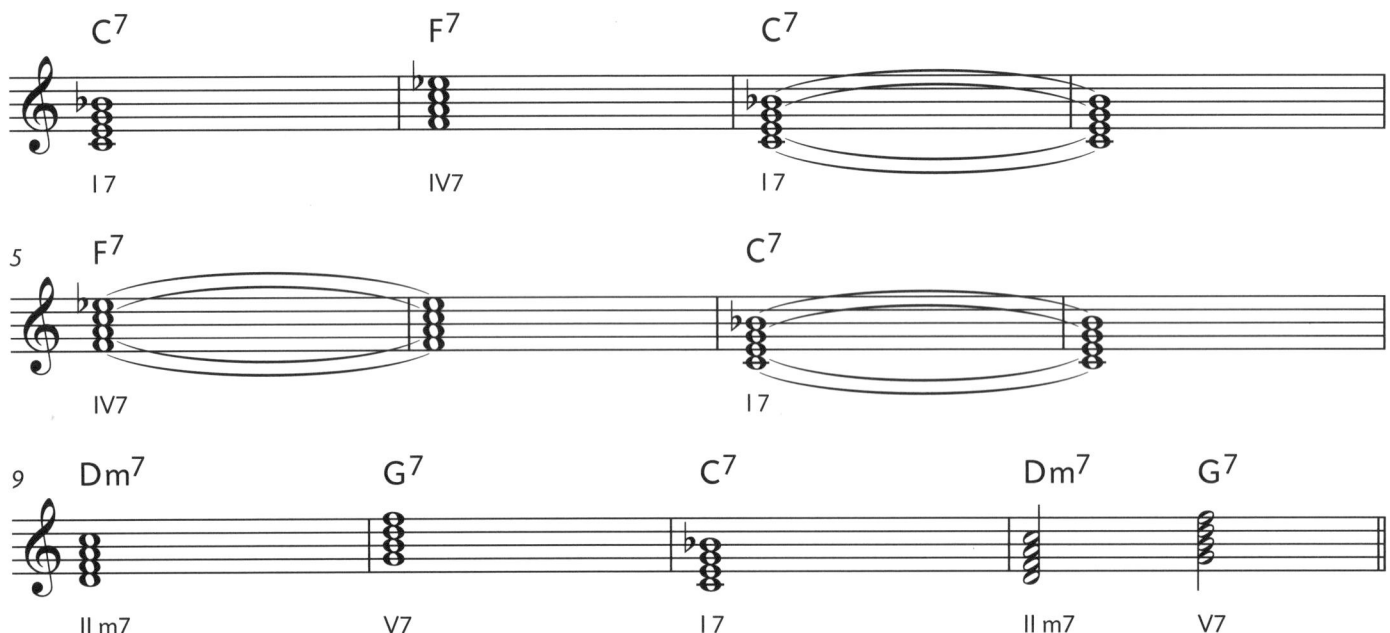

Blue Riff – Tenor Saxophone Solo

Gregory W. Yasinitsky

Most of the notes in this solo may be found in the C sweet blues scale and C standard blues scale.

Die meisten Noten in diesem Solo stammen aus der C-Bluestonleiter bzw. der „weichen" C-Bluestonleiter.

© 2016 advance music GmbH, Mainz

* A lick is a distinct phrase or an often played line. Many players develop their own set of signature licks.

* Ein Lick ist eine häufig gespielte oder besonders prägnante Phrase. Viele Jazzmusiker entwickeln eine Sammlung von persönlichen Licks.

7 "Blue Funk"

What to Play

When playing "Blue Funk," notes from the G standard blues scale and G sweet blues scale may be used for improvisation throughout.

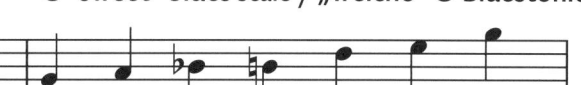

G standard blues scale / G-Bluestonleiter   G "sweet" blues scale / "weiche" G-Bluestonleiter

To begin with, you may wish to limit yourself to notes from one of these blues scales when improvising on "Blue Funk." As you become more experienced, you may alternate between the two blues scales whenever and wherever you like. *Combining these two scales into one composite scale does not work well, though.*

Why This Works

"Blue Funk" is a tune with a blues feeling in the key of G. It is not strictly a blues, but has a lot of blues elements. So blues scales may be used for improvisation throughout.

Learn to play the melody to "Blue Funk" by playing with the play-along recording. The recording alternates between passages in which the melody is played and passages in which only the rhythm section instruments–piano, bass and drums–are playing. *It is during these rhythm section passages that you may improvise. When the melody returns, you may join in with the melodic statement or continue improvising.*

Become familiar with the notes in both the standard and sweet blues scales, then try improvising–making up your own melodies and rhythms. **Be sure to improvise with confidence.**

When using the sweet blues scale, be careful of using B♮ against the C7 chords. The B will clash with B♭, the seventh of the C7 chord. So, playing B♭ against the C7 chords will be a better choice.

When using these two G blues scales for improvisation, it is not necessary to start on G. You may start on any note you want and play in any register you want. You are not limited to one octave. It useful to think of the notes in each scale as a set of pitches that may be played without a particular starting point or order. You may alternate between these two blues scales whenever and wherever you like. *Combining these two scales into one composite scale does not work well, though.*

7 „Blue Funk"

Welche Töne?

Beim Improvisieren zu „Blue Funk" können durchgängig Noten der C-Bluestonleiter und der „weichen" C-Bluestonleiter gespielt werden.

Vielleicht möchtest du dich beim Improvisieren zu „Blue Funk" erst einmal auf die Noten einer dieser beiden Bluestonleitern beschränken. Wenn du versierter wirst, kannst du zwischen den beiden Bluestonleitern abwechseln, wann und wo immer du willst. *Allerdings klingt es nicht gut, wenn man beide Tonleitern zu einer zusammengesetzten Tonleiter kombiniert.*

Warum es funktioniert

„Blue Funk" ist ein Stück mit Blues-Feeling in G. Streng genommen ist es kein Blues, enthält jedoch viele Blueselemente. Daher können zum Improvisieren durchgängig Bluestonleitern verwendet werden.

Du kannst die Melodie von „Blue Funk" lernen, indem du zur Playalong-Aufnahme mitspielst. In der Aufnahme wird zwischen Passagen, in denen die Melodie gespielt wird und Passagen, in denen nur die Rhythmusgruppe – Klavier, Bass und Schlagzeug – spielt, abgewechselt. *Bei den Passagen mit der Rhythmusgruppe kannst du improvisieren. Wenn die Melodie wiederkehrt, kannst du entweder die Melodie mitspielen oder weiterhin improvisieren.*

Lerne sowohl die Bluestonleiter als auch die weiche Bluestonleiter und probiere dann zu improvisieren, d. h. dir eigene Melodien und Rhythmen auszudenken. **Improvisiere auf jeden Fall selbstbewusst.**

Wenn du die „weiche" Bluestonleiter verwendest, solltest du aufpassen, wenn du ein B (H) zum C7-Akkord spielst. Das B (H) kollidiert mit dem B♭, der Septime des C7-Akkords. Daher ist es besser, ein B♭ zum C7-Akkord zu spielen.

Du musst nicht mit G beginnen, wenn du mit den Tönen der G-Bluestonleitern improvisierst, sondern kannst mit jedem beliebigen Ton anfangen und in jedem beliebigen Register spielen. Außerdem bist du nicht auf eine Oktave beschränkt. Stell dir die Töne der jeweiligen Tonleiter als Sammlung einzelner Töne vor, die keinen bestimmten Anfangspunkt und keine Reihenfolge haben.

There are unique expressive devices used by the best blues improvisers–scoops, bends, slurs and more. You should listen to great soloists using blues ideas to emulate the phrasing and inflections used by these accomplished jazz artists.

Du kannst zwischen den beiden Bluestonleitern abwechseln, wann und wo immer du willst. *Allerdings funktioniert es nicht gut, die beiden Tonleitern zu einer zusammengesetzten Tonleiter zu kombinieren.*

Es gibt viele Spieltechniken, die von den besten Bluesmusikern beim Improvisieren verwendet werden: Scoop, Bending, Slur etc. Hör dir bekannte Solisten an, die Bluesmotive spielen, um die Phrasierung und Verzierungen dieser versierten Jazzmusiker nachzuahmen.

About the Harmony

"Blue Funk" is not strictly a blues, but it includes blues ideas. The chord progression uses mainly dominant seventh chords, including dominant chords built on I and IV. These alternating dominant chords–G7, I and C7, IV7–add to the blues character of this tune.

All the notes in the melody may be found in the G sweet blues scale. There are also IIm7 to V7 chord progressions in bars 7 and 8 (in the first ending) and in bar 9 (in the second ending) that give the piece some jazz flavor.

Zur Harmonik

„Blue Funk" ist streng genommen kein Blues, enthält jedoch viele Blueselemente. Die Akkordfolge enthält viele Dominantseptakkorde, u. a. Dominantseptakkorde auf der I. und IV. Stufe. Diese abwechselnd gespielten Dominantseptakkorde – G7 (Akkord auf der I. Stufe) und C7 (Akkord auf der IV. Stufe) – verstärken den Bluescharakter des Stücks.

Alle Melodienoten stammen aus der „weichen" G-Bluestonleiter. Außerdem gibt es in Takt 7 und 8 (in Klammer 1) und in Takt 9 (Klammer 2) eine IIm7-V7-Verbindung, die dem Stück einen Jazz-Touch verleiht.

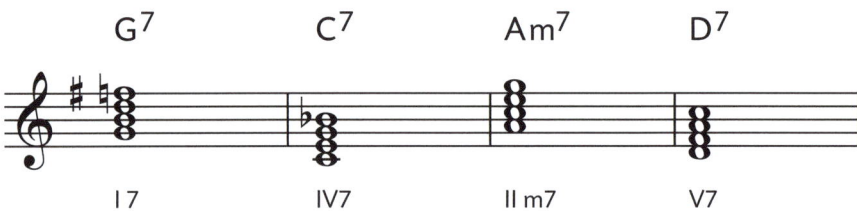

Blue Funk

Gregory W. Yasinitsky

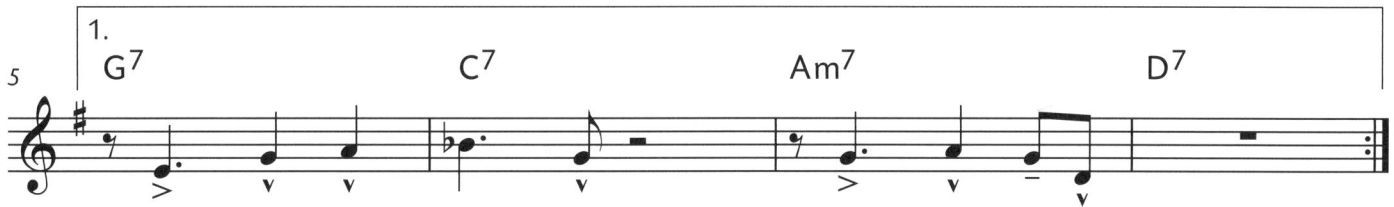

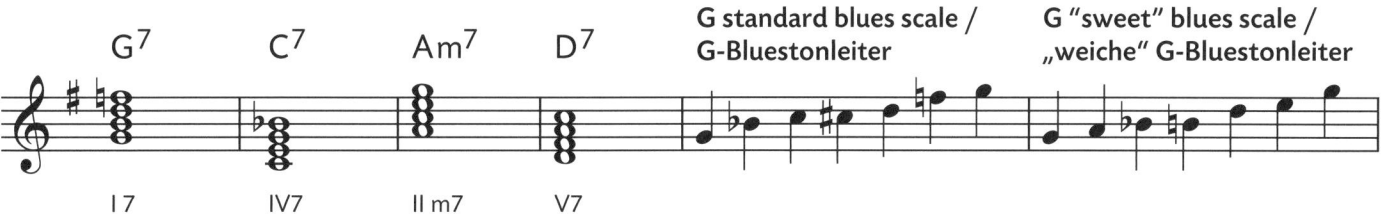

© 2016 advance music GmbH, Mainz

Blue Funk – Tenor Saxophone Solo

Gregory W. Yasinitsky

Most of the notes in this solo are from the G standard blues scale and the G sweet blues scale with an added chromatic tone (F#) leading to the root (G).

Die meisten Noten in diesem Solo stammen aus der G-Bluestonleiter bzw. der „weichen" G-Bluestonleiter, dazu gibt es noch einen Ton (F#), der chromatisch zum Grundton (G) führt.

© 2016 advance music GmbH, Mainz

Blue Funk – Trumpet Solo

Brian Ploeger

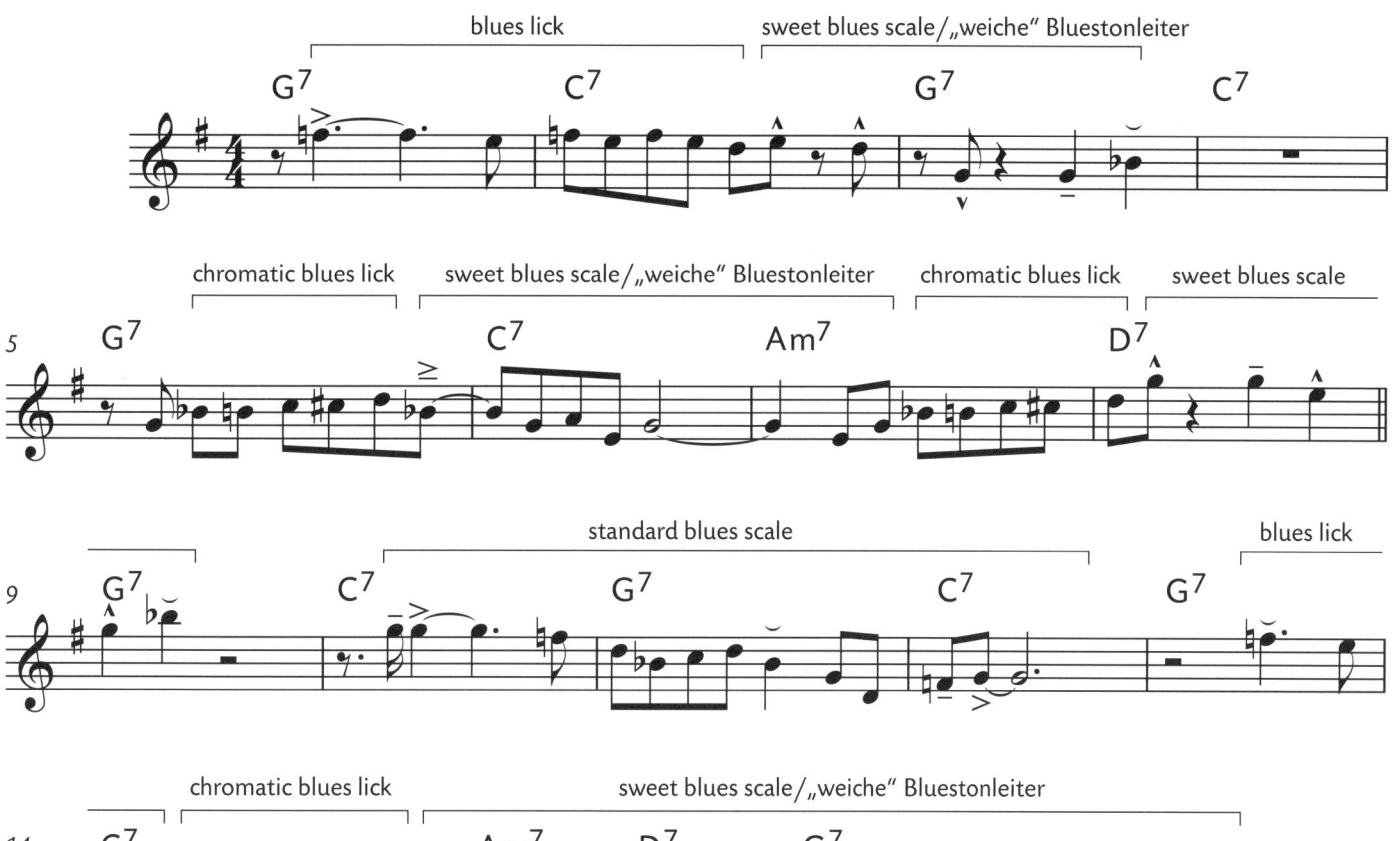

© 2016 advance music GmbH, Mainz

Most of the notes in this solo may be found in the G standard blues scale and G sweet blues scale with some additional blues licks.

Die meisten Noten in diesem Solo stammen aus der G-Bluestonleiter bzw. der „weichen" G-Bluestonleiter, dazu einige Blues-Licks.

8 "Feelin' Blue"

What to Play

When playing "Feelin' Blue," notes from the G standard blues scale and G sweet blues scale may be used for improvisation throughout.

To begin with, you may wish to limit yourself to notes from one of these blues scales when improvising on "Feelin' Blue." As you become more experienced, you may alternate between the two blues scales whenever and wherever you like. *Combining these two scales into one composite scale does not work well, though.*

G standard blues scale / G-Bluestonleiter   **G "sweet" blues scale / "weiche" G-Bluestonleiter**

Why This Works

"Feelin' Blue" is a blues tune composed in G. Because "Feelin' Blue" is a blues tune, blues scales may be used for improvisation throughout.

Learn to play the melody to "Feelin' Blue" by playing with the play-along recording. The recording alternates between passages in which the melody is played and passages in which only the rhythm section instruments–piano, bass and drums–are playing. *It is during these rhythm section passages that you may improvise. When the melody returns, you may join in with the melodic statement or continue improvising.*

Become familiar with the notes in both the standard and sweet blues scales. Once you are comfortable with the notes in these scales, try improvising–making up your own melodies and rhythms. **Be sure to improvise with confidence.**

When using the sweet blues scale, be careful of using B♮ against the C7 chords. The B will clash with the B♭, the seventh of the C7 chord. So playing B♭ against the C7 chords will be a better choice.

When using these two G blues scales for improvisation, it is not necessary to start on G. It useful to think of the notes in each scale as a set of pitches that may be played without a particular starting point or order. You may start on any note you want and play in any register you want. You are not limited to one octave. You may alternate between these two blues scales whenever and wherever you like. *Combining these two scales into one composite scale does not work well, though.*

There are unique expressive devices used by the best blues improvisers–scoops, bends, slurs and more. You should listen to great soloists using blues ideas to emulate the phrasing and inflections used by these accomplished jazz artists.

8 „Feelin' Blue"

Welche Töne?

Beim Improvisieren über „Feelin' Blue" können durchgängig Noten der G-Bluestonleiter und der „weichen" G-Bluestonleiter gespielt werden.

Vielleicht möchtest du dich erst einmal auf die Noten einer dieser beiden Bluestonleitern beschränken. Wenn du versierter wirst, kannst du zwischen den beiden Bluestonleitern abwechseln, wann und wo immer du willst. *Allerdings klingt es nicht gut, wenn man beide Tonleitern zu einer zusammengesetzten Tonleiter kombiniert.*

Warum es funktioniert

„Feelin' Blue" ist ein Bluesstück in G. Daher können die Bluestonleitern durchgängig zum Improvisieren verwendet werden.

Du kannst die Melodie von „Feelin' Blue" lernen, indem du zur Playalong-Aufnahme mitspielst. In der Aufnahme wird zwischen Passagen, in denen die Melodie gespielt wird und Passagen, in denen nur die Rhythmusgruppe – Klavier, Bass und Schlagzeug – spielt, abgewechselt. *Bei den Passagen mit der Rhythmusgruppe kannst du improvisieren. Wenn die Melodie wiederkehrt, kannst du entweder die Melodie mitspielen oder weiterhin improvisieren.*

Lerne sowohl die Bluestonleiter als auch die „weiche" Bluestonleiter. Wenn du die Noten dieser Tonleitern gut spielen kannst, probierst du zu improvisieren, d. h. dir eigene Melodien und Rhythmen auszudenken. **Improvisiere auf jeden Fall selbstbewusst.**

Wenn du die weiche Bluestonleiter verwendest, solltest du aufpassen, wenn du ein B (H) zum C7-Akkord spielst. Das B (H) kollidiert mit dem B♭, der Septime des C7-Akkords. Daher ist es besser, ein B♭ zum C7-Akkord zu spielen.

Du musst nicht mit G beginnen, wenn du mit den Tönen der G-Bluestonleitern improvisierst, sondern kannst mit jedem beliebigen Ton anfangen. Am besten stellst du dir die Noten der jeweiligen Tonleiter als Sammlung einzelner Töne vor, die keinen bestimmten Anfangspunkt und keine Reihenfolge haben. Du kannst mit jedem Ton beginnen und in jedem beliebigen Register spielen. Außerdem bist du nicht auf eine Oktave beschränkt. Du kannst zwischen den beiden Bluestonleitern abwechseln, wann und wo immer du willst. *Allerdings funktioniert es nicht gut, die beiden Tonleitern zu einer zusammengesetzten Tonleiter zu kombinieren.*

Es gibt viele Spieltechniken, die von den besten Bluesmusikern beim Improvisieren verwendet werden: Scoop, Bending, Slur etc. Hör dir bekannte Solisten an, die Bluesmotive spielen, um die Phrasierung und Verzierungen dieser versierten Jazzmusiker nachzuahmen.

About the Harmony

Blues has a unique harmonic structure, different from major and minor key harmony. There are many harmonic variations of blues. The most common form is twelve bars long and is referred to as a twelve-bar blues.

Blues progressions also generally include dominant seventh chords built on the first, fourth and fifth steps of the key (I, IV and V). Also in jazz, a blues progression will typically include a II-V progression in bars 9 and 10. These harmonic features may be found in the chord progression for "Feelin' Blue."

Study the chord progression and structure of "Feelin' Blue." *Work to memorize the progression.* Accomplished jazz musicians are expected to know how to construct typical blues progressions.

Zur Harmonik

Bluesstücke haben eine spezielle Harmonik, die sich von der Harmonik in Dur- und Molltonarten unterscheidet. Außerdem gibt es viele harmonische Variationen. Die geläufigste Blues-Form besteht aus zwölf Takten und wird als „zwölftaktiger Blues" bezeichnet.

Blues-Akkordfolgen enthalten üblicherweise Dominantseptakkorde auf der I., IV. und V. Stufe der Tonleiter. Im Jazz enthält eine Blues-Akkordfolge außerdem in Takt 9 und 10 eine II-V-Verbindung. Diese harmonischen Eigenschaften sind in der Akkordfolge zu „Feelin' Blue" zu finden.

Sie dir die Akkordfolge und den Aufbau von „Feelin' Blue" genau an. *Präge dir die Akkordverbindung gut ein.* Von versierten Jazzmusikern wird erwartet, dass sie typische Blues-Akkordverbindungen spielen können.

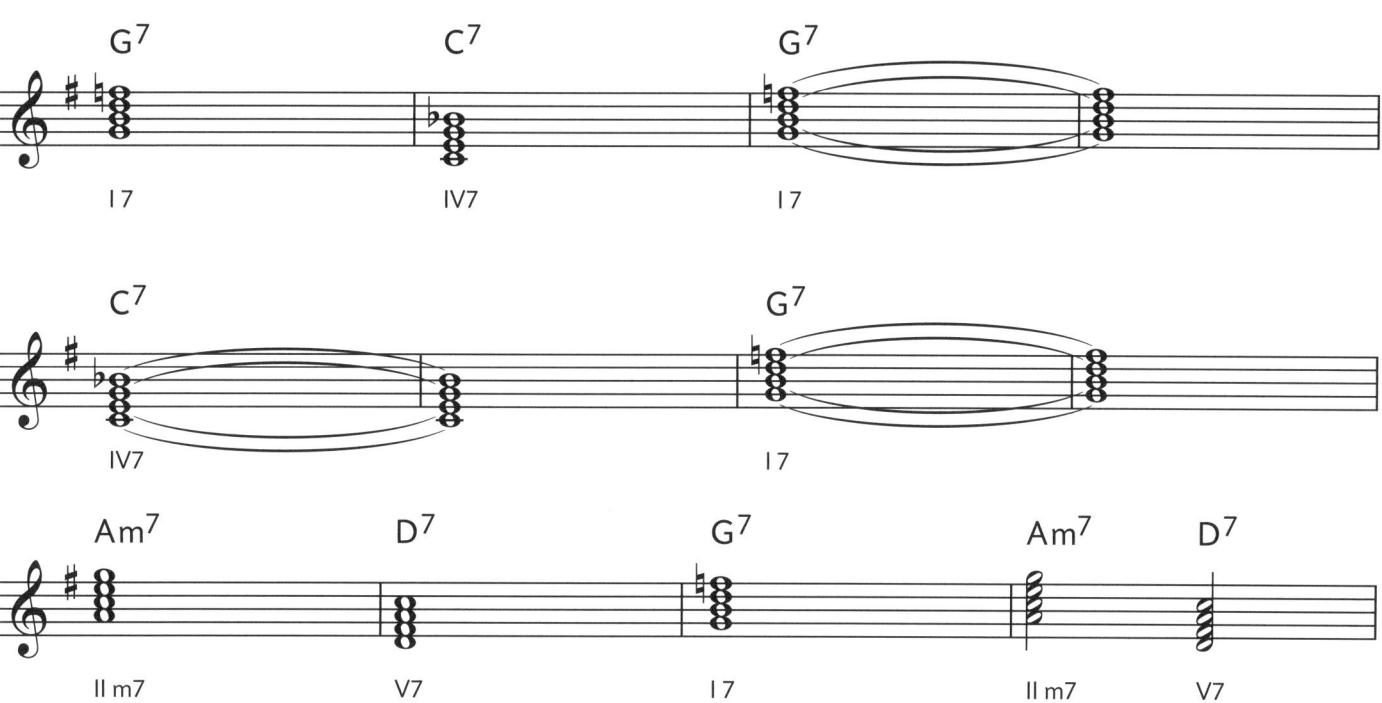

Feelin' Blue

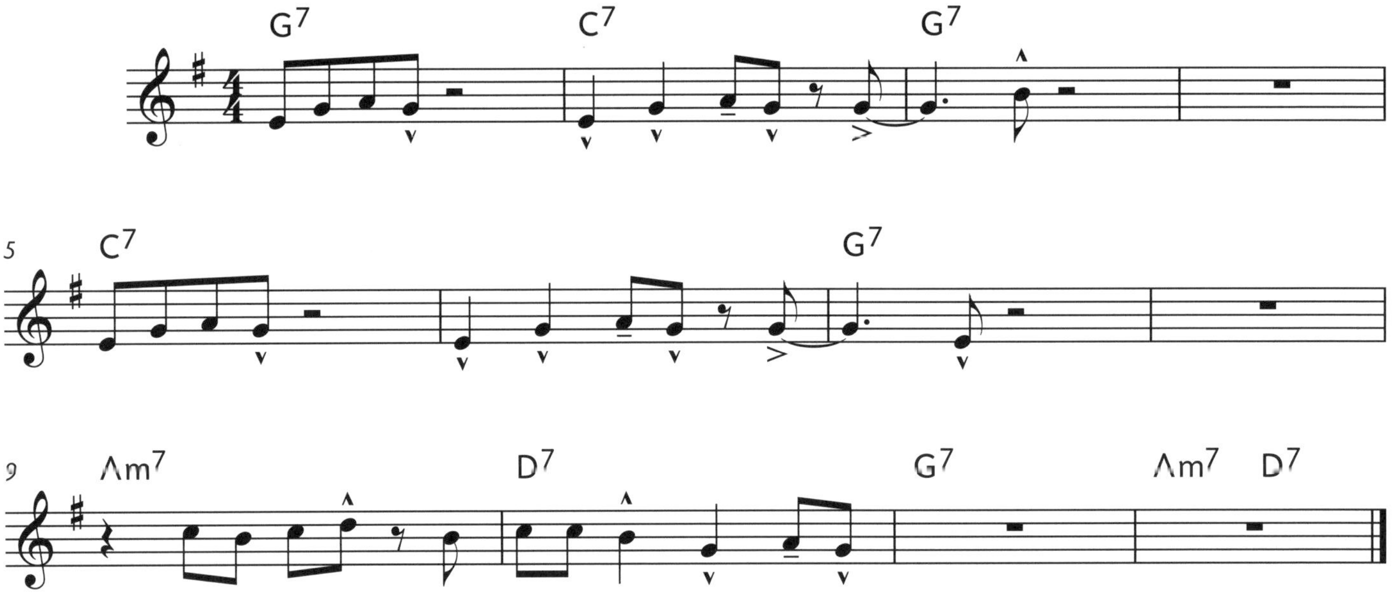

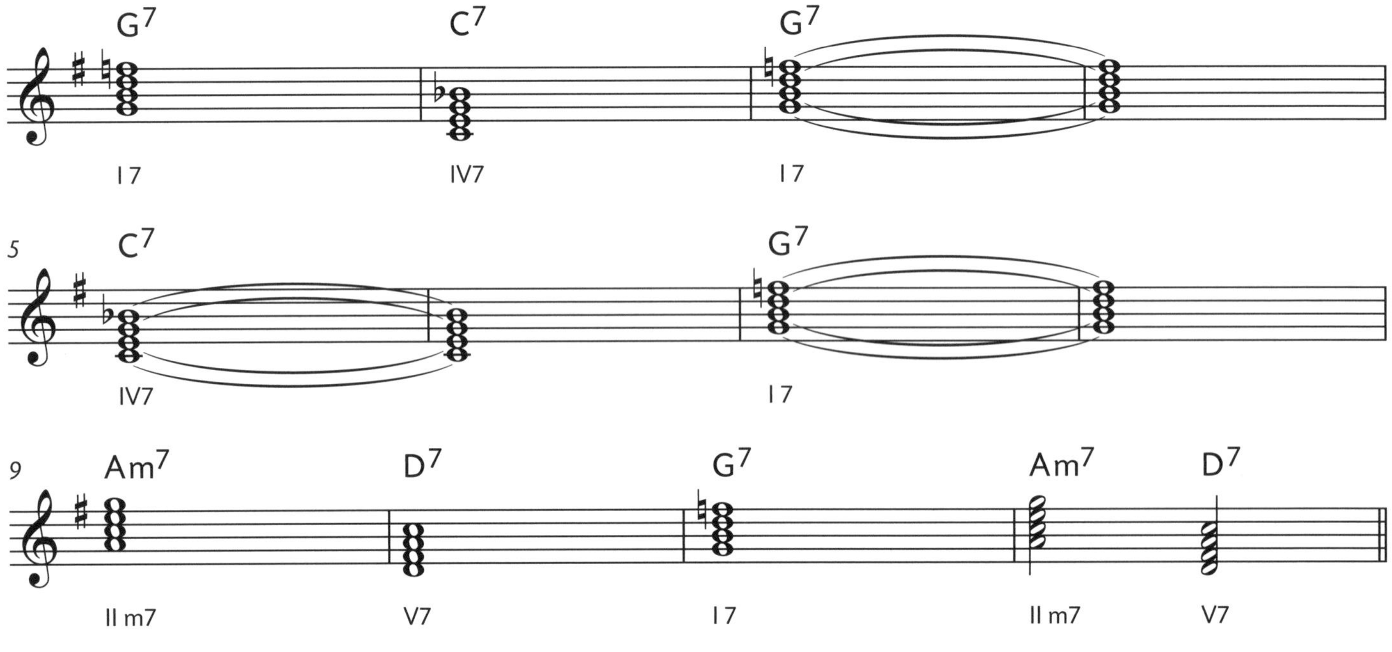

Gregory W. Yasinitsky

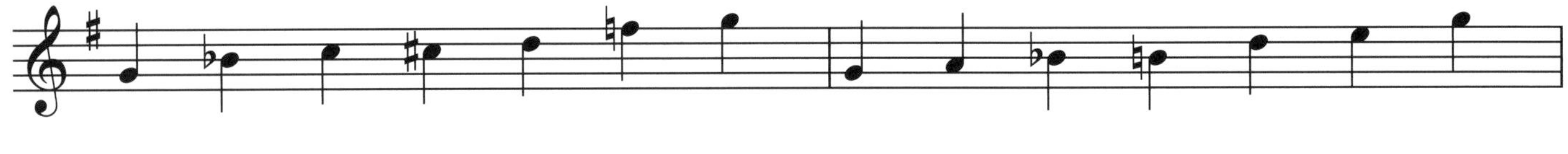

Feelin' Blue – Tenor Saxophone Solo

Gregory W. Yasinitsky

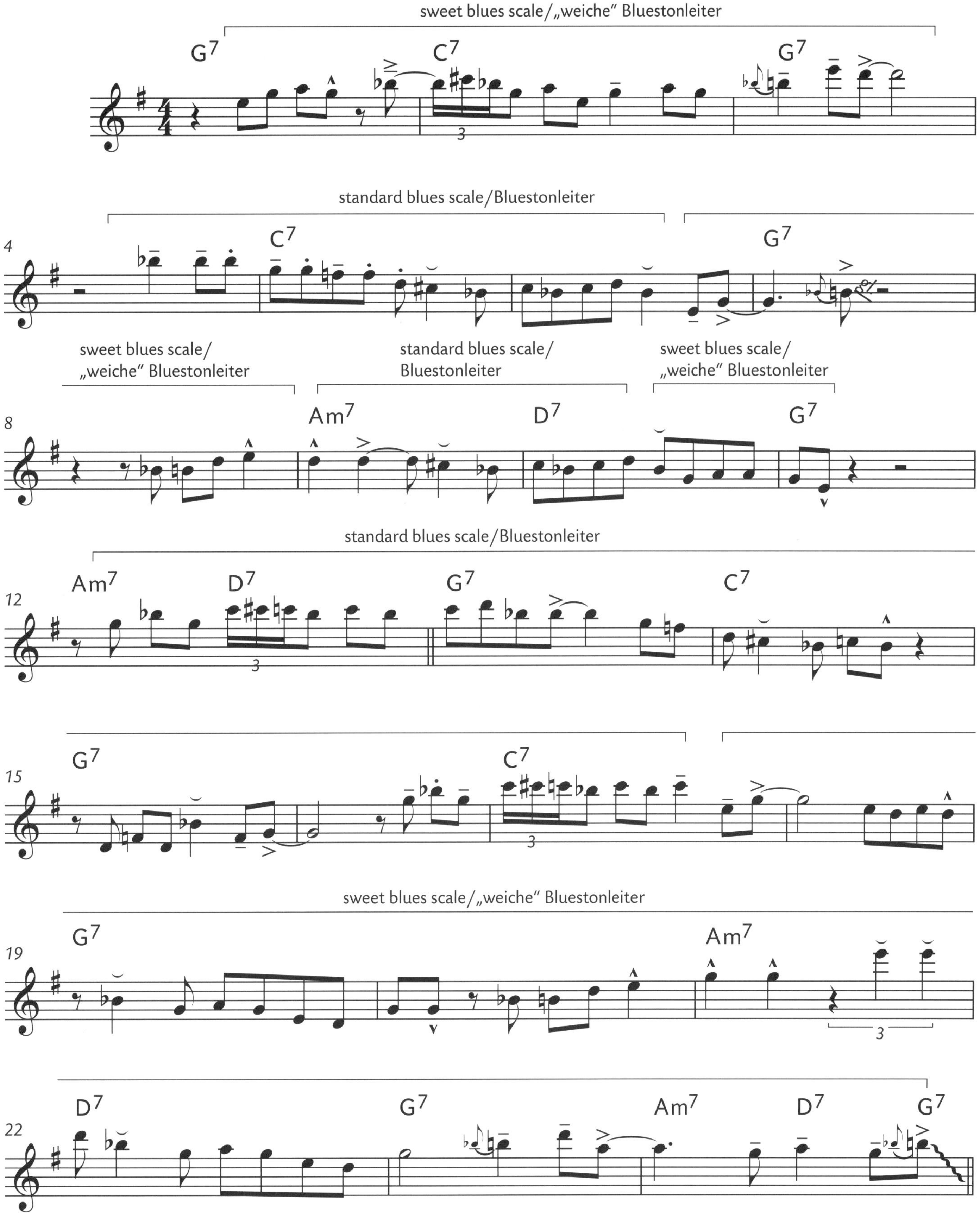

All of the notes in this solo are from the G standard blues scale and G sweet blues scale.

Alle Noten aus diesem Solo stammen aus der G-Bluestonleiter bzw. der „weichen" G-Bluestonleiter.

Feelin' Blue – Trumpet Solo

Brian Ploeger

Most of the notes in this solo may be found in the G standard blues scales and G sweet blues scale with an additional blues lick, some chromatic notes and an embellished G major scale.

Dieses Solo enthält Töne aus der „weichen" bzw. G-Bluestonleiter, ein Blues-Lick, einige chromatische Töne sowie eine G-Durtonleiter mit chromatischen Umspielungen.

9 "After the Spring"

What to Play

When playing "After the Spring," notes from the E natural minor and G major scales may be used for improvisation throughout. These two scales share the same notes because they are from relative keys—E minor and G major.

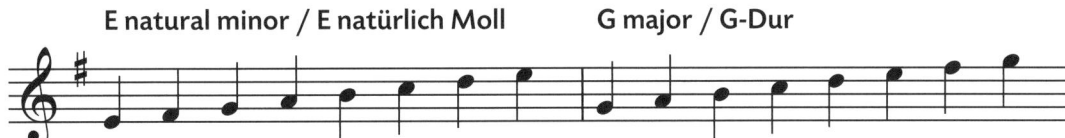

Why This Works

"After the Spring" is a tune which incorporates a number of the concepts from this book. The tune is mainly in E minor, but also has a section in G major. These are relative keys, so they share the same notes. This is why the notes from the E natural minor and G major scales work well throughout—all the notes in these scales are natural except for F♯.

Other Options

For the E minor sections of the tune, notes from the E harmonic minor scale may also be used. This scale is different from the E natural minor scale because the E harmonic minor scale includes a D♯ instead of a D♮.

The E standard blues scale also will work well throughout since the tune has a blues feeling.

Learn to play the melody to "After the Spring" by playing with the play along recording. The recording alternates between passages in which the melody is played and passages in which only the rhythm section instruments—piano, bass and drums—are playing. *It is during these rhythm section passages that you may improvise. When the melody returns, you may join in with the melodic statement or continue improvising.*

Become familiar with the notes in the E natural minor and harmonic minor scales, the G major scale and the E standard blues scale. Once you are comfortable with the notes in these scales, try improvising.

While improvising using notes from the E natural minor or harmonic minor scales, it is not necessary to start on E. When improvising using notes from the G major scale, again, it is not necessary to start on G. And also when improvising using notes from the E standard blues scale, it is not necessary to start on E.

When using the notes from each of these scales, you may start on any note you want and play in any register you want. You are not limited to one octave. Think of the notes in each of these scales as a collection of pitches, without a particular starting point or order. You may also use any rhythms that you like. **Be sure to improvise with confidence.**

Mach dich mit den Tönen von E natürlich und E harmonisch Moll, mit der G-Durtonleiter und der E-Bluestonleiter vertraut. Wenn du die Töne dieser Tonleitern gut spielen kannst, probierst du zu improvisieren.

Du musst nicht mit E beginnen, wenn du mit den Tönen von E natürlich oder harmonisch Moll improvisierst. Genauso wenig musst du mit G beginnen, wenn du mit den Tönen der G-Durtonleiter improvisierst. Und wenn du mit den Tönen der E-Bluestonleiter improvisierst, musst du auch nicht mit E beginnen.

Wenn du die Töne dieser Tonleitern verwendest, kannst du mit jedem beliebigen Ton anfangen und in jedem beliebigen Register spielen. Du bist nicht auf eine Oktave beschränkt. Am besten stellst du dir die Noten der jeweiligen Tonleiter als Sammlung einzelner Töne vor, die keinen bestimmten Anfangspunkt und keine Reihenfolge haben. Außerdem kannst du jeden beliebigen Rhythmus verwenden. **Improvisiere auf jeden Fall selbstbewusst.**

About the Harmony

The chord progression for "After the Spring" includes *chords in E minor* –

- **Em**, I
- **F♯m7(♭5)**, II
- **B7(♭9)**, V
- **Am**, IV

The alterations on the II and V chords indicate that the progression is in a minor key.

There is also a *section in G major* which includes the following chords –

- **Am7**, II
- **D7**, V
- **Gmaj7**, I.

The fact that the II and V chords are without alterations (plain) indicates that the progression is in a major key.

Zur Harmonik

Die Akkordfolge zu „After the Spring" enthält *Akkorde in E-Moll*:

- **Em**, Akkord auf der I. Stufe
- **F♯m7(♭5)**, Akkord auf der II. Stufe
- **B7(♭9)**, Akkord auf der V. Stufe
- **Am**, Akkord auf der IV. Stufe.

Die alterierten Töne der Akkorde auf der II. und V. Stufe weisen darauf hin, dass es sich um eine Akkordfolge in einer Molltonart handelt.

Außerdem gibt es einen *Teil in G-Dur*, der folgende Akkorde enthält:

- **Am7**, Akkord auf der II. Stufe
- **D7**, Akkord auf der V. Stufe
- **Gmaj7**, Akkord auf der I. Stufe.

Die Tatsache, dass die Akkorde auf der II. und V. Stufe keine alterierten Töne enthalten, bedeutet, dass es sich um eine Akkordfolge in einer Durtonart handelt.

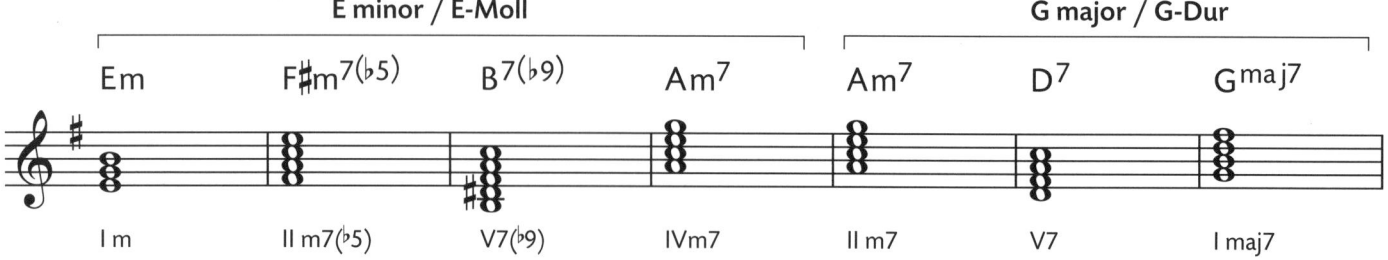

After the Spring

27

Gregory W. Yasinitsky

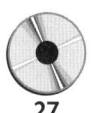

Bossa Nova

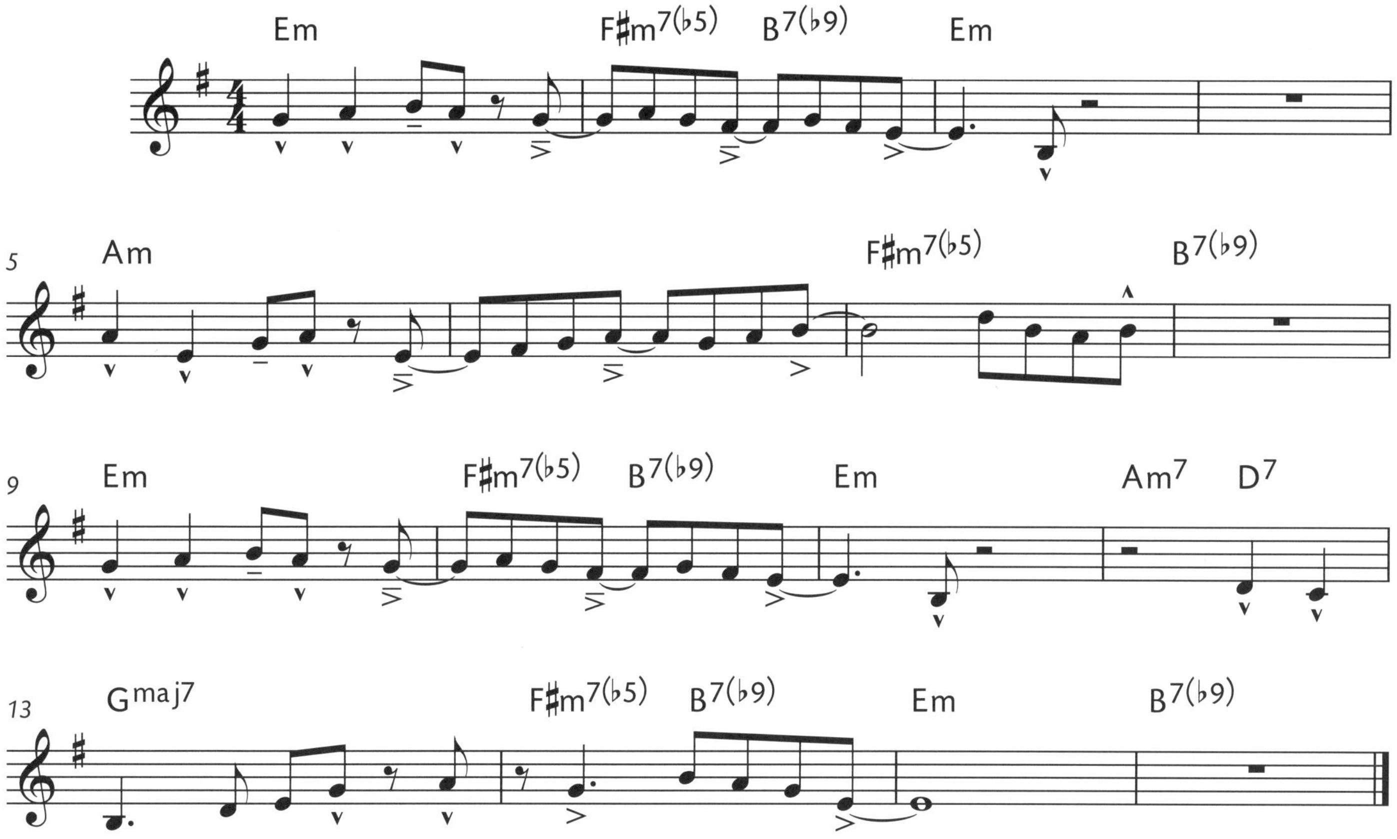

E Minor / E-Moll

G Major / G-Dur

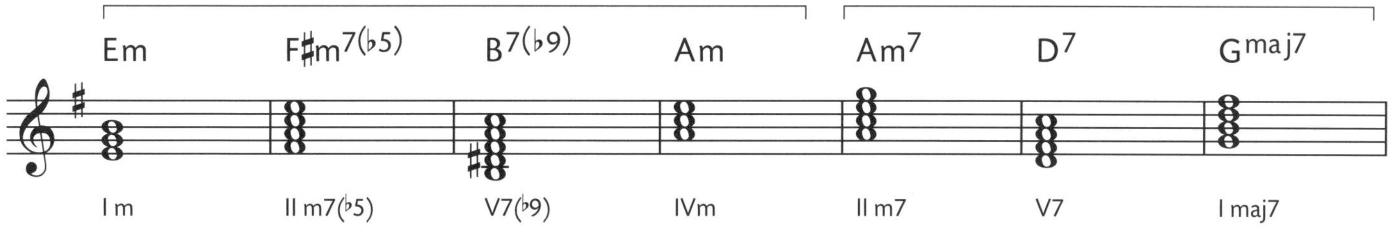

E natural minor / E natürlich Moll

E harmonic minor / E harmonisch Moll

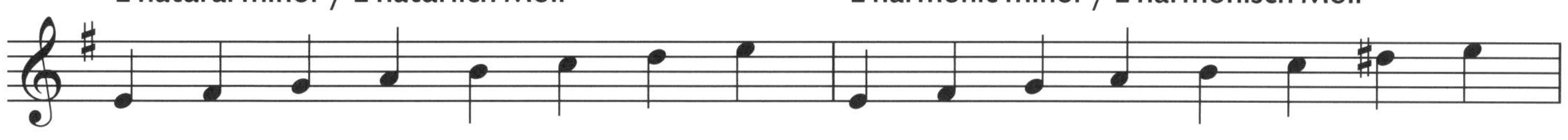

E standard blues scale / E-Bluestonleiter

G major / G-Dur

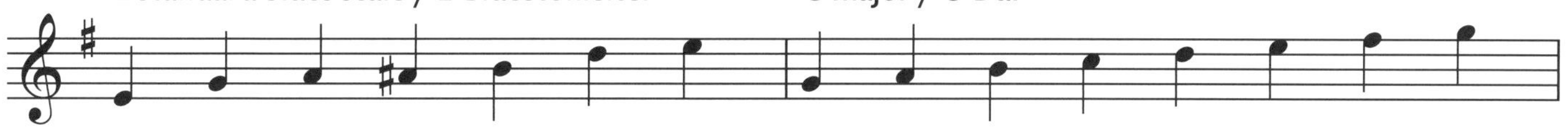

Tenor saxophonists should play this tune up an octave.

Tenorsaxophonisten sollten diese Melodie eine Oktave höher spielen.

After the Spring – Tenor Saxophone Solo

Gregory W. Yasinitsky

Most of the notes in this solo are from the E natural minor, E harmonic minor, G major and E standard blues scales with a few added chromatic tones.

Die meisten Noten in diesem Solo stammen aus E natürlich bzw. harmonisch Moll, G-Dur und der E-Bluestonleiter, dazu einige chromatische Töne.

After the Spring – Flugelhorn Solo

Brian Ploeger

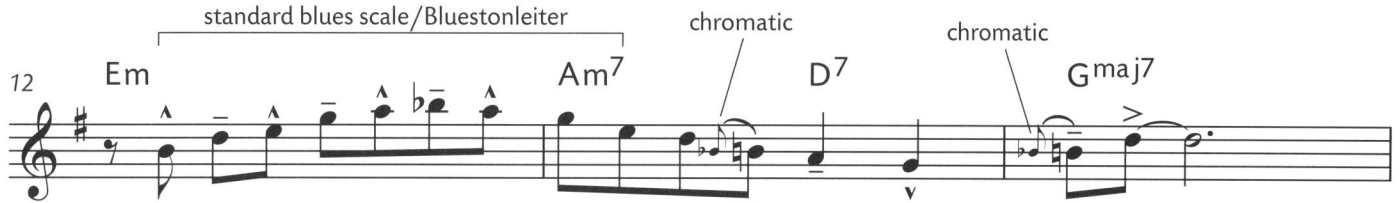

Most of the notes in this solo may be found in the E natural minor, G major and E standard blues scales with some added chromatic notes.

Die meisten Noten in diesem Solo stammen aus E natürlich Moll, G-Dur und der E-Bluestonleiter, dazu einige chromatische Töne.

10 Jazz Theory Guide

Key Signatures

Below are the key signatures for all major and minor keys.

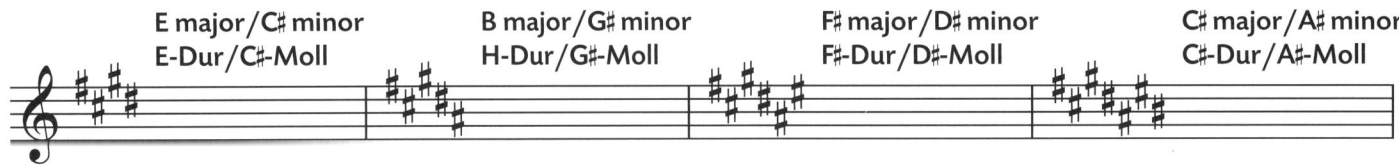

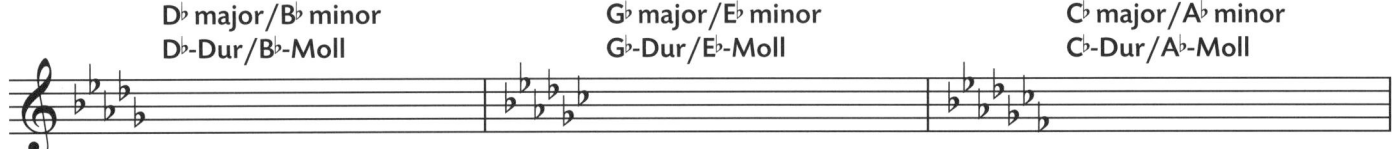

Scales

Below are the types of scales used in this book.

Major Scale

You can build a major scale by following this pattern:
whole step (W) • whole step • half step (H) • whole step • whole step • whole step • half step

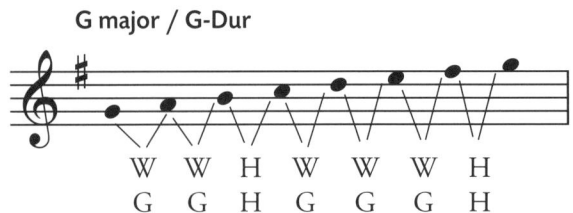

10 Jazz-Theorie-Leitfaden

Tonarten und Vorzeichen

Hier sind die Vorzeichen für alle Dur- und Molltonarten.

Tonleitern

Hier findest du die Tonleitern, die in diesem Buch verwendet werden.

Durtonleiter

Eine Durtonleiter wird stets nach dem folgenden Muster gebaut.
Ganzton (G) • Ganzton • Halbton (H) • Ganzton • Ganzton • Ganzton • Halbton

Natural Minor Scale

You can build a natural minor scale by following this pattern:
whole step • half step • whole step • whole step • half step • whole step • whole step

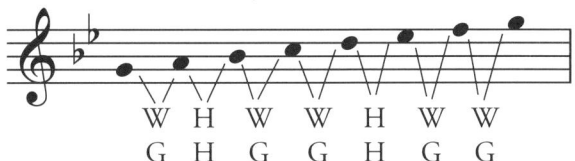

Harmonic Minor Scale

A harmonic minor scale can be built either by using the following pattern or by raising the seventh degree of a natural minor scale by a half step.
whole step • half step • whole step • whole step • half step • augmented second (whole step + half step) • half step

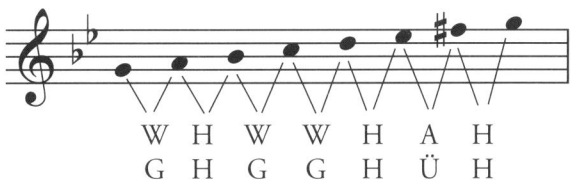

"Standard" Blues Scale

This is the pattern for a standard blues scale. Count from the root (1 = root, b3 = minor third, etc.).

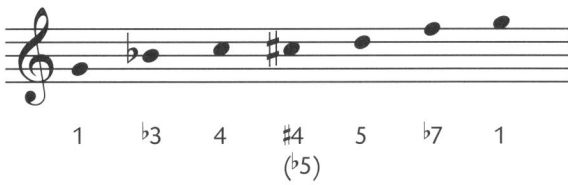

"Sweet" Blues Scale

This is the pattern for a "sweet" blues scale. Count from the root (1 = root, 2 = major second, etc.).

The G sweet blues scale has the same notes as the E standard blues scale, but starts on G.

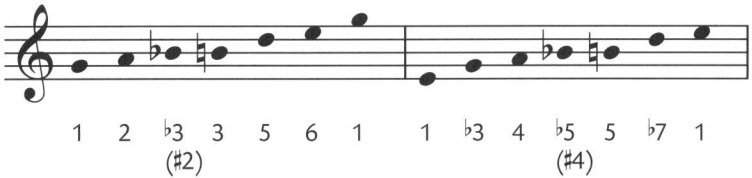

There are many other kinds of scales. Learn all you can about them.

Natürliche Molltonleiter

Eine natürliche Molltonleiter wird stets nach dem folgenden Muster gebaut.
Ganzton • Halbton • Ganzton • Ganzton • Halbton • Ganzton • Ganzton

Harmonische Molltonleiter

Eine harmonische Molltonleiter wird stets nach dem folgenden Muster gebaut. Sie unterscheidet sich von der natürlichen Molltonleiter durch eine um einen Halbton erhöhte siebte Stufe.
Ganzton • Halbton • Ganzton • Ganzton • Halbton • übermäßige Sekunde (Ganzton + Halbton) • Halbton

Bluestonleiter

Hier findest du das „Rezept" für die Bluestonleiter. Zähle vom Grundton aus (1 = Grundton, b3 = kleine Terz, usw.).

„Weiche" Bluestonleiter

Aus diesen Tönen besteht die „weiche" Bluestonleiter. Zähle vom Grundton aus (1 = Grundton, 2 = große Sekunde, usw.).

Die „weiche" G-Bluestonleiter enthält dieselben Töne wie die E-Bluestonleiter, beginnt jedoch mit G.

Es gibt noch viele andere Tonleitern. Du solltest möglichst viel über sie lernen.

Chords

Below are the types of chords and chord symbols used in this book.

Maj7, major seventh chord

A major seventh chord consists of a major triad (major third and perfect fifth) and the note a major seventh above the root of the chord.

The chord symbol for a major seventh chord consists of the note name of the root of the chord followed by the suffix maj7. Fmaj7 is the symbol for an F major seventh chord, B♭maj7 is the symbol for a B♭ major seventh chord.

m, minor chord

A minor chord (minor triad) consists of the root and the notes a minor third and perfect fifth above the root.

The chord symbol for a minor triad consists of the note name of the root of the chord followed by the suffix m. Fm is the symbol for an F minor triad, B♭m is the symbol for a B♭ minor triad.

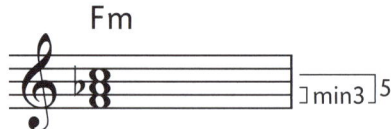

m7, minor seventh chord

A minor seventh chord consists of a minor triad (root, minor third and perfect fifth) and the note a minor seventh above the root of the chord.

The chord symbol for a minor seventh chord consists of the note name of the root of the chord followed by m7. Fm7 is the symbol for an F minor seventh chord, C♯m7 is the symbol for a C♯ minor seventh chord.

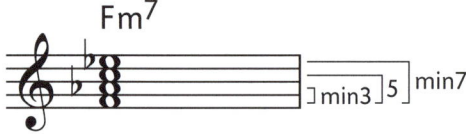

m7(♭5), minor seventh flat five chord (half-diminished chord)

A minor seventh flat five chord – also referred to as a half diminished chord with the symbol ø7 – consists of a diminished triad (minor third and diminished fifth) plus the note a minor seventh above the root of the chord.

Akkorde

Hier sind die Akkorde und Akkordsymbole, die in diesem Buch verwendet werden:

maj7, großer Durseptakkord, Major-7-Akkord

Ein Major-7-Akkord besteht aus einem Durdreiklang (Grundton, große Terz und reine Quinte) und der Note eine große Septime über dem Grundton des Akkords.

Das Akkordsymbol für einen Major-7-Akkord besteht aus dem Notennamen des Grundtons und dem Zusatz maj7. Fmaj7 ist also das Symbol für einen F-Major-7-Akkord, B♭maj7 ist das Symbol für einen B♭-Major-7-Akkord.

m, Mollakkord

Ein Mollakkord (Molldreiklang) besteht aus dem Grundton, der kleinen Terz und der reinen Quinte.

Das Akkordsymbol für einen Molldreiklang besteht aus dem Notennamen des Grundtons und dem Zusatz m. Fm ist das Symbol für einen F-Moll-Dreiklang, B♭m ist das Symbol für einen B♭-Moll-Dreiklang.

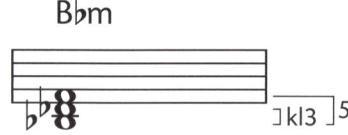

m7, kleiner Mollseptakkord, Minor-7-Akkord

Ein Mollseptakkord besteht aus einem Molldreiklang (Grundton, kleine Terz und reine Quinte) und der Septime über dem Grundton des Akkords.

Das Akkordsymbol für einen Mollseptakkord besteht aus dem Notennamen des Grundtons und dem Zusatz m7. Fm7 ist das Symbol für einen F-Mollseptakkord, C♯m7 ist das Symbol für einen C♯-Mollseptakkord.

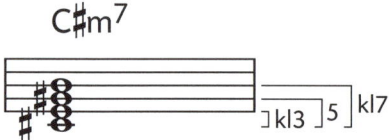

m7(♭5), kleiner Mollseptakkord mit verminderter Quinte, halbverminderter Septakkord

Ein Mollseptakkord mit verminderter Quinte – auch halbverminderter Septakkord mit dem Symbol ø7 genannt – besteht aus einem verminderten Dreiklang (Grundton, kleine Terz und verminderte Quinte) und dem Ton eine kleine Septime über dem Grundton des Akkords.

The chord symbol for a minor seventh flat five chord consists of the note name of the root of the chord followed by the suffix m7(♭5). Fm7(♭5) is the chord symbol for an F minor seventh flat five chord, G♯m7(♭5) is the chord symbol for a G♯ minor seventh flat five chord.

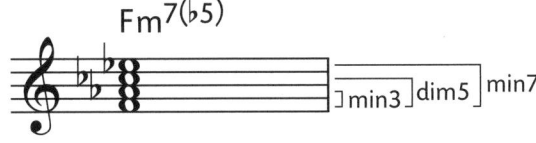

7, dominant seventh chord

A dominant seventh chord consists of a major triad (major third and perfect fifth) plus the note a minor seventh above the root of the chord.

The chord symbol for a dominant seventh chord consists of the note name of the root of the chord followed by the suffix 7. F7 is the symbol for an F dominant seventh chord, E♭7 is the symbol for an E♭ dominant seventh chord.

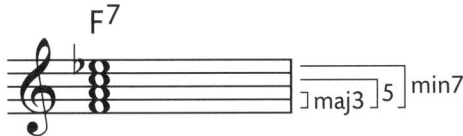

7(♭9), dominant seventh (♭9) chord

A dominant seventh flat nine chord consists of a major triad (major third and perfect fifth) plus the notes a minor seventh and minor ninth above the root of the chord.

The chord symbol for a dominant seventh flat nine chord consists of the note name of the root of the chord followed by the suffix 7(♭9). F7(♭9) is the symbol for an F dominant seventh flat nine chord, D7(♭9) is the symbol for an D dominant seventh flat nine chord.

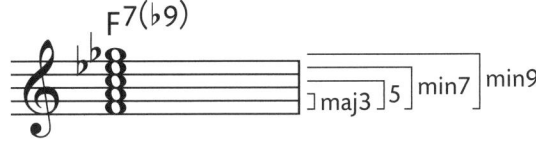

There are many other styles of chord symbols and many other types of chords. Learn all you can about them.

Das Akkordsymbol für einen Mollseptakkord mit verminderter Quinte besteht aus dem Notennamen des Grundtons und dem Zusatz m7(♭5). Fm7(♭5) ist das Akkordsymbol für einen F-Moll-Akkord mit verminderter Quinte, G♯m7(♭5) ist das Akkordsymbol für einen G♯-Moll-Akkord mit verminderter Quinte.

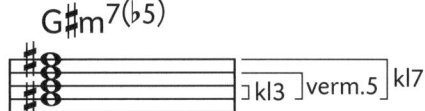

7, Dominantseptakkord

Ein Dominantseptakkord besteht aus einem Durdreiklang (Grundton, große Terz und reine Quinte) und dem Ton eine kleine Septime über dem Grundton des Akkords.

Das Akkordsymbol für einen Dominantseptakkord besteht aus dem Notennamen des Grundtons und dem Zusatz 7. F7 ist das Akkordsymbol für einen F-Dominantseptakkord, E♭7 ist das Akkordsymbol für einen E♭-Dominantseptakkord.

7(♭9), Dominantseptnonakkord, Dominantseptakkord mit kleiner None

Ein Dominantseptnonakkord (7-♭9-Akkord) besteht aus einem Durdreiklang (große Terz und reine Quinte) und der kleinen Septime und kleinen None über dem Grundton des Akkords.

Das Akkordsymbol für einen Dominantseptnonakkord besteht aus dem Notennamen des Grundtons und dem Zusatz 7(♭9). F7(♭9) ist das Akkordsymbol für einen F-Dominantseptnonakkord, D7(♭9) ist das Akkordsymbol für einen D-Dominantseptnonakkord.

Es gibt noch viele andere Akkordsymbole und viele andere Akkordtypen. Du solltest so viel wie möglich über sie lernen.

II-V Progressions in Major Keys

In a major keys, II chords are m7 chords, V chords are 7 chords (dominant seventh chords), and the distance between the roots of a II chord and V chord is up a perfect fourth or down a perfect fifth.

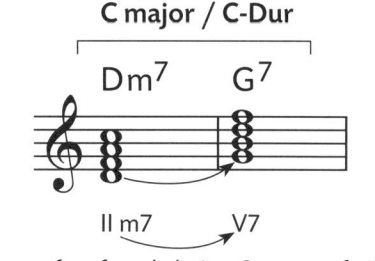

up a perfect fourth/reine Quarte aufwärts

In major keys, II-V progressions are "plain," without alterations.

II-V Progressions in Minor Keys

In minor keys, II chords are m7(b5) chords, V chords are 7(b9) chords and the distance between the roots of a II chord and V chord is up a perfect fourth or down a perfect fifth.

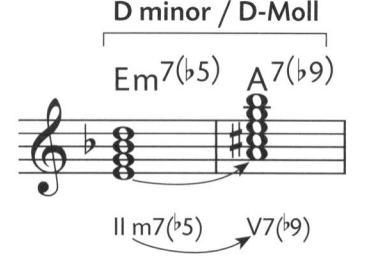

up a perfect fourth/reine Quarte aufwärts

In minor keys, the II and V chords are altered. These alterations indicate that the II-V is in a minor key.

II-V-Verbindungen in Durtonarten

In Durtonarten sind Akkorde auf der II. Stufe Mollseptakkorde und Akkorde auf der V. Stufe Dominantseptakkorde. Der Abstand zwischen dem Grundton des Akkords auf der II. Stufe und dem des Akkords auf der V. Stufe beträgt eine reine Quarte aufwärts bzw. eine reine Quinte abwärts.

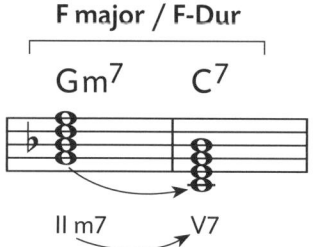

down a perfect fifth/reine Quinte abwärts

In Durtonarten enthalten II-V-Verbindungen keine alterierten Töne.

II-V-Verbindungen in Molltonarten

In Molltonarten sind Akkorde auf der II. Stufe Mollseptakkorde mit verminderter Quinte und Akkorde auf der V. Stufe Dominantseptnonakkorde. Der Abstand zwischen dem Grundton des Akkords auf der II. Stufe und dem des Akkords auf der V. Stufe beträgt eine reine Quarte aufwärts bzw. eine reine Quinte abwärts.

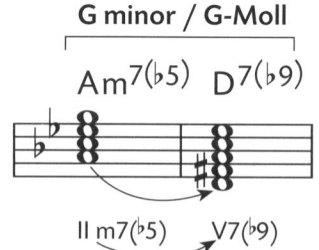

down a perfect fifth/reine Quinte abwärts

In Molltonarten enthalten die Akkorde auf der II. und V. Stufe alterierte Töne. Diese Alterationen zeigen an, dass es sich um eine II-V-Verbindung in einer Molltonart handelt.

CD Track List

1. Tuning Note, concert B♭ / Stimmton, klingend B♭
2. Tuning Note, concert A / Stimmton, klingend A
3. Getting Started, play along
4. Getting Started, tenor saxophone solo
5. Getting Started, trumpet solo
6. A Minor Change, play along
7. A Minor Change, tenor saxophone solo
8. A Minor Change, flugelhorn solo
9. The Key, play along
10. The Key, tenor saxophone solo
11. The Key, trumpet solo
12. It's All Relative, play along
13. It's All Relative, tenor saxophone solo
14. It's All Relative, flugelhorn solo
15. C Note, play along
16. C Note, tenor saxophone solo
17. C Note, trumpet solo
18. Blue Riff, play along
19. Blue Riff, tenor saxophone solo
20. Blue Riff, trumpet solo
21. Blue Funk, play along
22. Blue Funk, tenor saxophone solo
23. Blue Funk, trumpet solo
24. Feelin' Blue, play along
25. Feelin' Blue, tenor saxophone solo
26. Feelin' Blue, trumpet solo
27. After the Spring, play along
28. After the Spring, tenor saxophone solo
29. After the Spring, flugelhorn solo

Greg Yasinitsky, tenor saxophone • Brian Ploeger, trumpet and flugelhorn • Brian Ward, keyboard • F. David Snider, bass • David Jarvis, drums

Recorded, mixed and mastered in the Washington State University Recording Studio, David Bjur, engineer. Recordings produced by Greg Yasinitsky.

Greg Yasinitsky: Tenorsaxophon • Brian Ploeger: Trompete und Flügelhorn • Brian Ward: Keyboard • F. David Snider: Bass • David Jarvis: Schlagzeug

Aufnahme, Mixing und Mastering im Tonstudio der Washington State University. Toningenieur: David Bjur. Produziert von Greg Yasinitsky.